I0413795

EITHER CIVILIZED OR PHOBIC

Abhijit Naskar is one of twenty-first century's most influential minds in Neuroscience and an untiring advocate of global harmony and peace. He became a beloved best-selling author all over the world with his very first book "The Art of Neuroscience in Everything", that heralded the advent of a beautiful scientific philosophy. With various of his pioneering ventures into the Neuropsychology of religious sentiments, he has hugely contributed to humanity's attempt of diminishing religious differences, for which he is popularly hailed as a humanitarian who incessantly works towards taking the human civilization in the path of sweet general harmony.

EITHER
CIVILIZED
OR
PHOBIC

A TREATISE ON HOMOSEXUALITY

ABHIJIT NASKAR

Either Civilized or Phobic: A Treatise of Homosexuality

Copyright © 2017 Abhijit Naskar

This is a work of non-fiction

All rights reserved. No part of this publication may be
reproduced, distributed, or transmitted in any form or by any
means, including photocopying, recording, or other electronic
or mechanical methods, without the prior written permission
of the author, except in the case of brief quotations embodied
in critical reviews and certain other noncommercial uses
permitted by copyright law.

An Amazon Publishing Company, 1st Edition, 2017

Printed in United States of America

ISBN-13: 978-1546603030

Also by Abhijit Naskar

The Art of Neuroscience in Everything

Your Own Neuron: A Tour of Your Psychic Brain

The God Parasite: Revelation of Neuroscience

The Spirituality Engine

Love Sutra: The Neuroscientific Manual of Love

Homo: A Brief History of Consciousness

Neurosutra: The Abhijit Naskar Collection

Autobiography of God: Biopsy of A Cognitive Reality

Biopsy of Religions: Neuroanalysis towards Universal
Tolerance

Prescription: Treating India's Soul

What is Mind?

In Search of Divinity: Journey to The Kingdom of Conscience

Love, God & Neurons: Memoir of a scientist who found
himself by getting lost

The Islamophobic Civilization: Voyage of Acceptance

Neurons of Jesus: Mind of A Teacher, Spouse & Thinker

Neurons, Oxygen & Nanak

The Education Decree

Principia Humanitas

The Krishna Cancer

Rowdy Buddha: The First Sapiens

We Are All Black: A Treatise on Racism

The Bengal Tigress: A Treatise on Gender Equality

DEDICATION

Alan Mathison Turing (1912-1954)

"We can only see a short distance ahead, but we can see plenty there that needs to be done."

CONTENTS

1.Introduction

In the society of humans, what is normal and what is not, is defined by not the reality or the truth whatsoever. It is defined by the society's innate knacks and beliefs. In the eyes of the society, being normal does not always mean being yourself, rather it means putting up an act of what the society deems normal. And that's where, quite often, normalcy becomes not a proud possession of the individual self, rather the biggest head-ache of human life. Such a normalcy does not let a person manifest his or her true potential. It does not let an individual express and radiate the exuberance of his or her real identity. It does not let a person to truly live.

Keeping all this in mind, how can we, the so-called "sapiens" or "wise" beings, hail being normal to be something good and healthy. If such "normalcy" strips a person of his or her very identity, then we don't need such normalcy. If such normalcy rips apart a person's inner world instead of nourishing it, then we don't need such normalcy.

The conscientious individuals of the thinking society are the only people qualified to define the norms in the human society. Prejudices may have been the norms in the barbarian society of cave-people, but they have no place in the society of conscientious beings. Prejudices have no place in the society of humans. And any doctrine or norm that boastfully advocates for prejudicial barbarianism, must be discarded at ones.

Norms in the society of sapient beings are shaped by the perception of those beings. And these norms cannot be stagnant or rigid. They have to be ever-evolving. Otherwise, what one generation deems normal, may become an obstruction in the path of progress for the next generation. Norms are healthy as long as they do not drag the vehicle of progress backwards. Norms are good and healthy as long as they aid in the evolution of the human mind towards liberation. No liberation can be achieved without evolution. Change is a quintessential element of progress. Without change, progress is non-existent. Orthodoxy of any kind, be it in the line of religious doctrines or social norms, leads a species towards its extinction. Indeed, you either change or you get extinct.

2.Sexuality

Sex - this is the perhaps the most censored term in the world, and yet, it is also a term of immense ecstasy and unparalleled evolutionary significance. It is the phenomenon that enables a species to live on. However, in the human world, this term reaches new heights of gravitas beyond all its significance in the animal kingdom. In the human world, sex is the unique phenomenon that enables two separate beings become one all-pervading entity comprised of divine love.

In the human mind, true sexual intimacy is equivalent in all aspects to the transcendental experience of meeting God. That is why there are some traditions in the world that hail sexual union as the means to attain God or Divinity. Sex is not just about going in or letting in, it is really about welcoming your dearly beloved into the deepest regions of your psyche which are inaccessible to anybody else. Sexual intimacy is not the destination, it is the path - the path that leads to mental union.

Physical union is merely the means to mental intimacy. In the unification of two minds, orientation of sexuality is irrelevant. From a humanistic as well as medical standpoint, mental unification is the purest manifestation of love, which is independent of sexual identity. It does not matter what the dumb, ignorant and primitive cave-people of the society deem a sin - the fact remains, that sexual orientation is no measure for judgement either about love, parental ability or anything else. The only measure of romantic love is care and understanding. There is nothing else.

Sexual orientation does not define love, but one's perception of sexual orientation does define whether that person is a civilized being or just pretending to be one. It is as simple as this - either you are homophobic or you are a human - you cannot be both. Similarly, either you are Islamophobic or you are a human - you cannot be both. Either you are a fundamentalist or you are a human - you cannot be both. Either you are racist or you are a human - you cannot be both. Either you are sexist or you are a human - you cannot be both. Homophobia, Islamophobia, racism, sexism and fundamentalism - all these are signs of barbarianism. And as such they have no place in the modern society, if we are to hail our society as modern.

True humans of the civilized society are above all prejudices. So, either you are civilized, or phobic (not in medical terms). Being civilized does not mean wearing nice clothes - being civilized means being conscientious - it means being rational - it means having cortical control over the limbic responses of prejudices.

Remember, love has no gender - compassion has no religion - character has no race. And sexuality is a fundamental element of love, or to be specific, romantic love. In fact, in the early phase of love, it is sexuality that drives a person down the road of pair-bonding, which over time leads to true love.

In the beginning of a romantic relationship, it is actually the evolutionary drive for sexual intimacy that guides a person in his or her romantic endeavors. In most cases, this process takes place in the human psyche without the person even being aware of it. Let me simplify. It means that even though the actual experience during those early days of a relationship, when you actually start to fall in love with someone, mostly consists of sweaty palms, butterflies in the stomach, sleepless nights of tossing and turning, thumping heart, loss of appetite and a sense of euphoria, all of that experience is actually your brain's way of telling you that that special someone is a healthy fertile peer to mate with.

Hence it may feel totally surreal and non-sexual in most cases, but if you peel back the layers of those symptoms, deep down you will find the force of libido functioning at full throttle to get you a suitable mate. Perhaps this scenario could most beautifully be demonstrated with the memories of my days at the university, before I quit. In this context, let me bring up an excerpt from my memoir "Love, God & Neurons: Memoir of a scientist who found himself by getting lost."

I kept attending the classes, regardless of their uselessness. They were like, one brainless robot regurgitating a stream of preprogrammed data, which the other young robots were gobbling with their eyes and shoving inside their hippocampus (the brain's memory formation center).

I kept attending the classes for one single reason – a mature radiant girl, potentially filled with triggers that would evoke a hormonal tsunami inside my entire neuroanatomy. Her name was Sally Saha. But I preferred to call her by her nick name Pickoo. Just by calling her by her nick name used to give me a sensation of intimacy. And even our roll numbers in the class were intimate, hers was four and mine was three.

I was one of the backbenchers in the class. And she was one of the front-sitters. Every day, I would go inside the class after twenty minutes of bus journey from the dorm, only to sit at the back and keep staring like a birdwatcher at the beautiful blue jay in the front row, while my fellow backbenchers made fun of me. Every day for hours I used to drink from her radiant fountain of sweetness, which poured my veins with soothing warmth. Her face was like cocaine that affected the dopamine system of my neurobiology. This made my brain filled with dopamine, giving me the feeling of overwhelming warmth and joy, which is exactly what happens under the influence of cocaine. Forget engineering, I was simply happy by looking at her all day, then come to the dorm room and take pleasure in recollecting every single detail of her face.

Almost half a year at the university went like this. Then one day, quite out of the blue, she caught me by surprise while I was coming out of the building. We had already gained knowledge about each other from our classmates. And as it turned out, we both were from the same city. And both of us used to go home almost every weekend and then attend classes back on Monday.

She approached me with an unforeseen offer, which was totally platonic on her side. She simply needed a person - a friend to go home with. At that moment, she was more mature than me in the emotional realm, while I on the other hand was simply a country boy who never had a relationship before and was drowning in love with her.

So, there my months-long birdwatching at fifteen feet of distance, suddenly turned into sitting next to the brown blue jay for a four hours long heavenly journey. We hopped on a tri-cycle together at the university gate, to get to the Burdwan train station. And the whole three hour journey on the train to Howrah (a city adjacent to Calcutta) became the most romantic journey of my teenage years, even though the romance was all on my side of neuropsychology. Even from a platonic perspective she was the most unromantic person on earth, because most part of the journey she would just put her damn earplugs on and act as if I wasn't there.

But who the hell was analyzing her behavior! The very region of analyzing things in my brain was turned off like a blackout during a Coronal Mass Ejection or Solar Storm. And I was overwhelmed with feelings rising from a highly active limbic system, trigged by the close proximity of the girl I been admiring for months. Upon reaching our destination, the Howrah station, we had to take a bus to enter our city. So, there was half an hour more of sitting next to the silent actress until we had to part our ways.

While talking about the theory of relativity Albert Einstein once said:

"Put your hand on a hot stove for a minute, and it seems like an hour. Sit with a pretty girl for an hour, and it seems like a minute. That's relativity."

This is exactly what became of those four hours. Four whole hours felt like four tiny minutes after we parted our ways upon reaching Calcutta. It was like four delightful minutes in heaven...

Before going our separate ways that colorful weekend, we exchanged numbers. It was probably the happiest day of my university life. I went home, filled with a subconscious inkling of an imminent relationship. Every time when I remembered our bodies carefully caressing each other while sitting in the bus side by side, a rush of endorphins turned my inner cosmos into the most beautiful abode of love and passion. Like an actual boyfriend in a romantic relationship I saved her number in the classic Nokia flip phone that I had, with a special Bengali romantic song as a ringtone. It was all simple madness, exactly what everyone feels in the early phase of euphoric love.

Love begins with the stage of subconscious primitive lust and attraction. I'm saying primitive because at this very early stage there is really no difference between primitive man and modern man. The bodily characteristics of a person such as, how hot they are, poke the level of sex hormones (testosterone and estrogen), cortisol and pheromones. Lust is initiated at this stage through the physical attraction and flirting. In my case the flirting was simply about lending a friendly hand and showing that I deeply cared. This is an evolutionary behavior of man that biologically enables him to find a healthy and fertile mate.

A woman triggers a storm of hormonal surges in the male brain with her beauty and attractiveness, which quite subconsciously signals the male brain, that she would make a perfectly fertile mate. While on the other hand, a man triggers similar emotional surges in the female brain with his nurturing nature, which subconsciously signals the female mind that he would make a caring partner and nurturing father.

Following the cue of lust, the major attraction symptoms kick in, which are usually known as the symptoms of love, such as sweaty palms, tremors in the whole body, restlessness, loss of appetite and sleep, thumping heart, butterflies in the stomach etc. Such symptoms occur because the body is flooded with neurochemicals like Dopamine, Cortisol, Norepinephrine and Phenylethylamine (PEA). This is the very first stage of love that gives rise to a crazy euphoric sensation. The passion of this euphoric stage creates the feeling of exhilarating happiness that is often unbearable and certainly indescribable.

It is not until the euphoria wears off, that the deepest stage of love starts to prevail that is the attachment phenomenon. And the chemicals that make this possible are Oxytocin, Vasopressin and Endorphins. As time goes by, the crazy love sensation diminishes and the feeling of closeness and attachment grows and prevails till the last breath of life.

Naturally, over time my neurochemicals compelled me to grow a sense of intense attachment with Sally. After that weekend, we started to share our journey home almost every week. Even though I was not her actual boyfriend, to all the people in the class, we appeared as a couple. And it was a fascinating feeling, when jealous singles stared at us with a burning envy. Here one thing to mention is that even though the early stage of love is directly connected to libido, in most cases, the sensation itself doesn't manifest in a sexual manner. Nature programmed the neurobiological processes of early love to appear as something beyond the primitive sexual cravings of the genitals.

So, from an evolutionary standpoint, it all leads to copulation and reproduction, but from the perspective of the individual who has recently fallen head over heels in love with someone, it is mostly about a sensation of warmth and delight, and rarely of sexual nature. Similar was my experience. It was all ecstatic and never sexual, even though, that ecstasy was Nature's way to trick my mind into ultimately having Sally as my mate. It was all an evolutionary mechanism to ultimately drive me inside her.

- *Love, God & Neurons: Memoir of a scientist who found himself by getting lost*

What our ancestors learnt about love and relationship is intricately encoded in our genetic blueprint. And that blueprint enables us to do all sorts of crazy things in the pursuit of love. Love literally makes us illogical, because in the throes of new romance, the brain's department of analysis, that is the Prefrontal Cortex, turns a little less active. This makes us cognitively blind towards our dearly beloved, especially in the early days of a relationship. This entire process of becoming illogical actually helps two individuals to sustain the relationship long enough to get to know each other without getting ticked off by the imperfections. In a relationship, communication, consummation and closeness collectively contribute to the formation of a mental bond between two separate beings.

Ultimately it is all about survival of the species through reproduction. Here one might wonder, if the purpose of sexuality is reproduction then how does homosexuality make sense! Well, it is not really about reproduction, but about survival of the species. Reproduction serves that purpose of survival through heterosexuality, and so does homosexuality. My proposition here is, just like the inability to reproduce, uncontrolled reproduction in time leads to the extinction of a species. Hence, homosexuality evolved in the animal kingdom including humans as a population-control mechanism. Mother Nature selected this biological variation to keep the population on earth in check. That's the evolutionary reason behind the existence of same sex orientation, and as for its neurological underpinnings, we shall dive deep into it in the next chapter.

Now let's focus our attention on the society's stigmatized notion of homosexuality. I agree that it is the responsibility of us scientists to act as the official truth-seekers of humanity and thereafter make humanity acquainted with the truth. But let me ask you this. What kind of primitive stone-age society do we live in, where humans are seen as not humans but some inferior creatures with no dignity simply because their sexual orientation is different from what is hailed as normal!

In reality, here it's not the homosexuals, who are inferior creatures with no dignity, but those who hail them as such are. Humans who discriminate other humans based on sexual identity, gender, religion or race are no humans at all. They are in all aspects mindless apes with no other purpose of life but to eat, reproduce, defecate and attempt to drag the human civilization back to stone-age.

I am a human being, and as such, I proudly speak about acceptance of all humans as equal, because that is the only quality that defines the true essence of being human. But acceptance does not mean accepting those who disregard humans on the basis of race, religion and sexual orientation. Accepting evil is worse than committing evil. You must – I repeat – you must, as a human being, stand up on the side of humanism, against barbarian inhumanism, for it is your action, that shall determine whether your children shall live in a world of peace and harmony or a world of chaos and discriminations. You my friend, have the power in your hands to change what others chose to ignore. Those who remain silent in the face of evil are not even worth the title of "coward" for cowardice is a human quality. They are insignificant creatures who have nothing to offer the world they live in. Silence helps discriminations. Hence, you must speak up. Speak up – from the bottom of your heart – speak the truth – because those who speak the truth have nothing to fear. Unleash the truth and it will defend itself like a lion.

We don't yet live in a civilized world no matter how much we boast that we do. Nevertheless, the world can become genuinely civilized if the humans in it become conscientious enough to question even their own inner prejudices. The moment you learn to question your own actions and emotional responses, is the moment when the world truly begins to become civilized.

A civilization is built upon the edifice of genuine human minds, not the primitive and deluded minds of barbarian apes, who in most cases read one book of opinions written hundreds or thousands of years ago and think that they have factual answers to all the questions in the world.

Remember, shallow intellect is worse than ignorance. Ignorance can be treated with knowledge, but shallow intellect, that is illusion of knowledge, is untreatable and quite dangerous to the progress and wellbeing of humanity.

The world needs love – the world needs care – the world needs understanding. Are you able to love my friend? Then love your fellow humans. Are you able to care my friend? Then care for your neighbors? Are you able to understand my friend? Then try to understand the strangers you meet. Understand but do not judge. And if you must, then judge by the content of their character and nothing else, for it is the character that becomes immortal, not a race, a gender, a religion or an orientation of sexuality. If your nationality is lost, nothing is lost – if your religion is lost, nothing is lost – if your ethnicity is lost, nothing is lost – but if your character is lost, then you are more lost than Donald Trump.

Now, forget baby Trump and let's talk about sexuality. Sexuality is a quintessential part of your personality. And the elements of sexuality and relationship differ vividly between men and women. For example, women tend to emphasize committed relationships as a context for sexuality more than men do. In a study, when young adults were asked to define sexual desire, men were more likely than women to emphasize physical pleasure and sexual intercourse. In contrast, women were more likely to romanticize the experience of sexual desire. Young women's definition of sexual desire is often expressed as *"longing to be emotionally intimate and to express love for another person"*. Which means, to a woman sexual intimacy is more a tool to get mentally close to her partner than merely a means to physical pleasure, unlike a man, to whom sexual intimacy is more about physical stimulation than mental communion.

Studies on human sexual behavior reveal that compared with women, men have more permissive attitudes toward casual premarital sex and toward extramarital sex. The size of these gender differences is relatively large, particularly for casual premarital sex. Similarly, women's sexual fantasies are more likely than men's to involve a familiar partner and to include affection and commitment. In contrast, men's fantasies are more likely to involve strangers, anonymous partners, or multiple partners and to focus on specific sex acts or sexual organs.

And these gender differences do not only exist in the psyche of heterosexual individuals, but also, they are quite significantly seen in homosexual partners. For example, like heterosexual women, lesbians tend to have less permissive attitudes toward casual sex and sex outside a primary relationship than do gay or heterosexual men. Also like heterosexual women, lesbians have sex fantasies that are more likely to be personal and romantic than the fantasies of gay or heterosexual men. Lesbians are more likely than gay men to become sexually involved with partners who were first their friends, then lovers. Gay men in committed relationships are more likely than lesbians or heterosexuals women to have sex with partners outside their primary relationship.

In summary, women's sexuality tends to be strongly linked to a close relationship. For women, the best context for pleasurable sex is a committed relationship. This is less true for men. To put it simply, a woman desire for sex not to get physical pleasure, but to intimately feel the person she loves – to get closer to her partner at a spiritual level.

Also, there is an element of aggression in male sexuality, which is characterized by a feeling of power and dominance. In contrast, it is comparatively less present in female sexuality. The element of aggression makes men in heterosexual relationships to be commonly more assertive than women and take the lead in sexual interactions. During the early stages of a dating relationship, men typically initiate touching and sexual intimacy. In ongoing relationships, men report initiating sex about twice as often as their female partners. To be sure, many women do initiate sex, but they do so less frequently than their male partners. The same pattern is found in people's sexual fantasies. Men are more likely than women to imagine themselves doing something sexual to a partner or taking the active role in a sexual encounter.

In this context, let me provide you with a tactic which would be helpful if either you or your partner lacks confidence and self-esteem in social situations. If one lacks confidence and self-esteem in social life, then taking the lead in conjugal activities with one's partner would act as reinforcement of the confidence and esteem at a neurological level. Which means, if you lack confidence then talk to your partner about it and take the lead in bed. Similarly, if your partner lacks confidence then let her or him take the lead more often. The confidence gained in bed over time gets imposed on the person's personality and begins to radiate in all aspects of life.

In human sexual behavior there is a fascinating phenomenon called Sexual Plasticity. In comparison with male sexuality, female sexuality tends to have greater plasticity. Which means, women's sexual beliefs and behaviors can be more easily shaped and altered by cultural, social and situational factors.

The frequency of women's sexual activity is more variable than men's. If a woman is in an intimate relationship, she might have frequent sex with her partner. But following a breakup, she might have no sex at all, including masturbation, for several months. Men show less temporal variability. Following a breakup, men may substitute masturbation for interpersonal sex and so maintain a more constant frequency of sex. There is also growing evidence that women are more likely than men to change their sexual orientation over time. In a study, more than 25% of 18 to 25 years old women who initially identified as lesbian or bisexual changed their sexual identity during the next 5 years. Changes such as these are less common for men.

A person's sexual attitudes and behaviors are substantially responsive to social and situational influences. Such factors as education, religion, and cultural influence are more strongly linked to women's sexuality than to men's. For example, moving to a new culture may have more impact on women's sexuality than on men's. Also, quite interestingly the experience of higher education provides another illustration. For example, college education is associated with more liberal sexual attitudes and behavior, but this effect is greater for women than for men.

Even more striking is the association between college education and sexual orientation. Completing college doubled the likelihood of a man identifying himself as gay or bisexual. However, college was associated with a 900% increase in the percentage of women identifying as lesbian or bisexual.

Diverse lines of our scientific research have identified consistent male-female differences in sexual interest, attitudes toward sex and relationships, the association between sex and aggression, and sexual plasticity. Understanding these differences can help you have a more pleasurable experience of love making. Understanding these differences will allow you to have a more fulfilling relationship with your partner. And as far as sexual intimacy is concerned, good sex is about knowing each other's deepest and kinkiest desires.

Many intellectual idiots of the society with their metaphysical vanity boastfully comment that love and lust are two very different things. They consider love to be something sacred, whereas lust is sinful. And that is the most delusional notion about love that you can ever hear. Love and lust are not separate experiences, they are intertwined at a physiological level. The brain circuits of lust and sexual arousal are intertwined with the brain circuits of love. In fact, without the preliminary subconscious kick of lust, no love can ever even set off.

So, regardless of all our pretenses, deep within, we are still unconsciously the same old cave-people. And there is nothing wrong in accepting our innate biological instincts. On the contrary, problems occur when we do not accept our real selves. Being aware of our deepest biological instincts gives us an evolutionary advantage of programming our own responses and behaviors for a better outcome in our daily life.

The best illustration of instinctual imprints in brain circuits can be more easily found in men than women. Brain scan studies have shown that even a neutral scenario of a conversation between a man and a woman triggers sexual regions in the observer male brain giving rise to thoughts of potential sexual rendezvous. Whereas a woman only perceives the scenario as it is – just a simple communication between two people.

The male and female brain circuits below the belt are distinctively unique in their own way. And the clearest signs of such gender differences can be seen in the time required for orgasm. On average it takes a woman three to ten times longer than a man to reach orgasm. There is a biological reason behind it. After all, the evolutionary purpose of coitus is to make babies. So, when a woman reaches climax after her man has already ejaculated, it is more likely for her to conceive. However, orgasm is not compulsory for a woman to get pregnant, but it definitely helps.

Since we are talking about orgasm, let's explore the erotic world of female orgasm. Clitoris is the queen of this erogenous domain. The tip of the clitoris which is called "glans" has more than 8000 sensory nerve endings which communicate directly with the pleasure center of a woman's brain. So, whenever those nerves along with the surrounding vaginal tissues are stimulated by the passion of a man or a vibrator, they evoke electrochemical impulses. And once these impulses reach the threshold, they trigger the torrents of feel-good and bonding neurochemicals such as oxytocin, dopamine and endorphins.

To talk about orgasmic stimulation, I must clear the air about a classic misperception. I am talking about the eternal battle between "vaginal orgasm" and "clitoral orgasm". It all began with the flawed thoughts of Sigmund Freud. He may have illuminated the world of psychoanalysis to a great extent, but in many cases his ideas actually were filled with flaws. In simple terms, he thought that all psychological problems are born out of sexual repression. As a modern day neuroscientist, let me clarify something. Physiology and psychology are not at all separate from each other. Rather they are deeply intertwined.

Sigmund Freud, the assumed father of psychoanalysis neither had a clear perception of the anatomy of human brain, nor did he have flawless notion of the anatomy of clitoris. But, his ideas had such an intuitive appeal that many of the words he used, infiltrated popular parlance. To be honest, alongside his contribution to the psychoanalysis community, many of his theories actually ruined the sex life of many women. For nearly a century his theories of fornication made women believe that they were not quite real women if they only had clitoral orgasm. Over time we neuroscientists have discovered that the clitoris is the major organ of orgasm in the female body. And the surrounding area of the vaginal opening assists in reaching climax.

So, the bottom-line is, there is no such thing as "vaginal orgasm" vs. "clitoral orgasm". The entire ring of tissues that surrounds the vaginal opening is connected to the clitoris by nerves and blood vessels. Ultimately all these tissues together are responsible for the female orgasm. This entire erogenous zone is often referred to as the "ring of fire".

Now, once the ring of fire has done its job by fulfilling a woman's orgasmic pleasure, her brain is engulfed with dopamine and oxytocin which make her want to cuddle, whereas inside the male brain, the story is completely different. Many women complain that their men tend to fall asleep right after sex. Well, that is actually true, but the reason is not what women think. This specific phenomenon is called "post-coital narcolepsy". Oxytocin is released in both the male and female brain during and after sex promoting a warm sensation in the body. But while in women it induces the urge to cuddle and talk, inside the men's head post-coital burst of oxytocin triggers the sleep center inside the hypothalamus. So, it is not at all true that a man doesn't want to stay awake and cuddle for some time after sex. It is his biology that automatically induces him to sleep. However, we don't yet have the answer to why does Oxytocin work as a sedative only in men and not women?

Sexual bliss is such a state of your mind, that there is no place for anxiety, fear or analytical thinking. So, in order to get a burning turn on, the brainy regions of the brain must be turned off. Researchers have found that it only takes five minutes of casual conversation with a sexy lady for a man's testosterone level to go sky high. And testosterone is the prime driver of the sexual arousal circuits in the male brain.

For a woman it takes a few extra steps to warm up for a sexual encounter. Unlike the male brain, the female brain requires much more than just a hot looking person to get aroused. Her entire biology must be relaxed and cozy in order to have a go into the erotic domain of sexual bliss. Specifically, a hot bath, a good foot rub, chocolates and flattering words before sex unplug the woman from her daily stress and make her ready for the sexual ecstasy. And off course, sexual ecstasy is contagious. So, when the woman is swept off her feet in bed, her man automatically feels the sensuality bursting within his veins. As if some kind of unknown and mysterious force-field overwhelms them for limitless eternity.

All it takes for a man to have a full erection is visualization. If a man perceives the potential for any kind of sexual reward in his field of vision his brain sends signal through his spinal cord to the penis. Thereafter blood rushes to the penis making it erect. Here is a beautiful contrast between sensitivity of the tip of the penis and the tip of the clitoris. The 8000 nerve endings of the clitoris make the tip of it more and more sensitive as the woman gets excited, but the penile sensitivity has a different story. Researchers at McGill University have discovered that the tip of the penis gets less and less sensitive as a man gets more and more aroused.

As blood rushes to the responsible crucial parts of the body such as the penis, clitoris and breasts, we'd discover, brain's fear center amygdala that can interfere in the blissful communion slowly goes dark. Then as the penile thrust begins, the Nucleus Accumbens (the pleasure center of the brain) in both sexes, lights up like a thousand suns. Symptoms that go along with this heavenly experience such as sensual moaning, quickened breath, trembling, muscle spasms and throbbing heart make you feel on top of this world. And upon reaching orgasm, a tsunami of oxytocin rushes in both the male and female bodies. Right after reaching climax, a glow of contentment radiates from a woman's glistening skin, as the post-coital rush of oxytocin makes her chest and face blush by expanding the blood vessels. But even one clumsy move during sex by the man, can bring the female amygdala back into action, ruining all the sexual interest. Ergo, orgasm goes out of the window.

In our understanding of the true purpose of female orgasm we are way behind male orgasm. The male orgasm is pretty straightforward. There is no two way about it. But there is lot of hot debate in the scientific community about the purpose of the female orgasm. Alongside the cold perception that there is no actual purpose at all, we do have several hypotheses that give us some ideas to what might the purpose of the female orgasm be. So far, the major hypotheses on this matter are: pair-bonding, mate-choice, enhanced fertility and by-product hypothesis.

The by-product hypothesis is the coldest among all of them and doesn't hold much water. It states that female orgasm has no evolutionary function, existing only because women share some early ontogeny with men.

The pair-bonding hypothesis suggests that the orgasm is a way of communication between the satisfaction of the female and male body. Hence it builds intimacy in a relationship.

Along comes the mate-choice hypothesis. It airs the idea that the female orgasm inspires a woman's mind to cherry-pick the best genetic bet for her offspring. In simple terms, the man who gives a woman intense orgasms, naturally becomes her subconscious choice.

But biologically the most evident hypothesis is the enhanced fertility hypothesis. There have been several studies published on this idea. During orgasm the uterine contraction sucks up the sperm through the cervical mucus barrier. In some rare cases the uterine suction had been so strong that it literally pulled off the man's condom. Research has shown that when a woman achieves orgasm any time between one minute before and forty-five minutes after her man ejaculates, she pulls significantly more sperm than orgasm-less coitus. So, technically that's the reason why men are biologically designed to ejaculate way earlier than women. It's all about the survival of a species through procreation. This was the first priority of Mother Nature while she was designing the humans so craftily over millions of years. Ergo, she made the experience of sexual communion the most ecstatic experience on planet earth. It feels so damn good, that we just want to do it over and over again.

A successful orgasm in a woman involves a lot of psychological factors as well, which often get in the way of having a healthy sex life. The female brain is a high-performance emotion engine that retains emotional memories both good and bad much longer than the male brain.

Past experiences of a woman's life make a deep impact over her mental state. And this can interfere in her sexual ecstasy, making it hard for her to have a blissful orgasm.

For example, if a woman had been sexually abused in her childhood or if in her past sexual relationship she had been forced to do something against her will, then such traumatic experience can lead to an unsatisfied sexual life. So, in this kind of circumstances things must be handled with utmost care and concern. Often a combination of sex therapy and trauma therapy proves very effective in such situations. However, the most effective treatment on this matter can provided by the woman's partner, which is to let her speak her heart out.

The very rudimentary element of trauma therapy is to vent all the emotions connected to that experience. Once all the repressed and unshared junk is thrown outside the mind, the woman would feel much better. So, once the foundation of trust in a relationship becomes strong enough, it is much healthier to share all your past memories with each other. Keeping secrets is a kind of emotional repression that actually requires some engagement of the conscious mind in both the man and woman. And over time as the burden of repression gets heavier, it'd start to affect a relationship in a very bad way. So, remember to make time for venting repressed emotions to your trusted partner every now and then. This would not only strengthen your relationship but also lead to mental and physical wellbeing for you and your partner.

Now let's have a look at some serious psychological factors involved in men's performance in bed. The first thing that many of the women wonder, is *"what is it with men and blowjob!"* Does this mean, men like their package inside women's mouth more than they like it inside their vagina? Technically the answer would be "Yes". And there is a simple biological reason behind it. The sensitive part of a penis works in a different way than the tip of the clitoris. In women, during penetrative sex, the "ring of fire" (clitoris and the surrounding vaginal tissues) slowly gets more and more warmed up sending jolts of electrochemical signals to the brain's pleasure center. But in men, the glans of the penis gets less and less sensitive during penetration to reduce the pain of intercourse.

And Mother Nature's bizarre naughtiness is seen when a woman's soft lips, wet tongue and fingers slowly start to caress a man's penile glans. It sends him into an inexplicable paradise as he receives a heightened sensitivity of the glans. Oral sex increases the sensitivity of the tip of the penis in such a way that doesn't occur inside the vagina.

Now let's shed some light over some of the classic male worries concerning sex. Everybody knows about the male concern about size and along with that there is one more worry, which is often called "performance anxiety". In the beginning of sex life, many men worry about their performance in bed. They are concerned about their sexual impression way more than women are aware of. Whether they'll get fully erect! What if they come way too soon! These thoughts frequently float around inside a man's head right before sex. Men need to be relaxed just like women in order to have a proper high performance erection. And daily physical workout can increase men's sexual efficacy. Ergo, maintaining a healthy physique is one of the means to have an excellent love life with bed-bursting sex.

Along comes the size concern. A lot of men wish they had a bigger penis. Research has shown that the average erect penis size ranges from 5.5 to 6.2 inches, which is more than enough for a satisfactory coitus. However, quite surprisingly many men even go through surgery in order to add a few centimeters to their package. The fact is, women are not particularly bothered by the size of the penis. If anything, then it's about how long a man can sustain his erection. And the manly physical features that can turn on a woman are body symmetry, muscles, jawline, smile etc.

Women are either subconsciously or consciously attracted to men who elicit maturity, confidence and sociability. And in case of choosing a partner to raise a family with, research has shown that facial hair in men attracts the mother in a woman planning for babies. The subconscious part of the mind makes a woman prefer a man with facial hair as the father of her progeny over a clean-shaven man. However, there is no specific scale for physical attractiveness. It can only be perceived, not measured. And how we perceive attractiveness or beauty of the opposite sexes depends on our brain circuits. As I have said in my book "The Bengal Tigress: A Treatise on Gender Equality" -

Beauty is an illusion.

Beauty is an illusion, created by Mother Nature to drive the human species in the path of reproduction. In reality, beauty is irrelevant to human life, especially in a relationship. What you today perceive as beautiful and special, over time, becomes not so special. That's how the human brain works. It is not beauty that keeps a relationship alive, it is attachment. Without attachment, a naked body is merely a lifeless sex toy.

A man who wakes up to a pair of double D breasts of his wife every morning, is neurologically destined to get used to them, regardless of their size. This is called "Habituation". But this process of habituation does not say anything about the love and care between two persons in a committed relationship.

Love is not the primeval surge of libidinal lust that a person receives when meeting a suitable partner for the first time. Love in the truest sense of the term is born much later in a relationship, when both sides get to the know the truest selves of each other. Sexuality, or to be specific, sexual intimacy, simply acts as an important ingredient in the making of the delicious cuisine of true love. True love is not found – it is built. And sex aids in the process.

The most important chemicals in the formation of true love aided by sexuality are Oxytocin and Vasopressin. They play a critical role in forming a concept of our partner whom we want to be with. They appear to build a strong profile of the mating partner through odor. The odor comes to be associated with a pleasurable and rewarding encounter with a particular partner. The same works in the visual domain. Oxytocin is not only responsible for the bonding of couples but also it is involved in maternal love towards a baby, whereas vasopressin is responsible for the commitment of the male towards his mate.

But the brain region activation in women that correlates with maternal love is not identical to the one with romantic love. An interesting distinction lies in the strong activation of fusiform gyrus that is involved in the attention to faces in maternal love. This counts for the importance of reading children's facial expressions to ensure their well-being. This leads to the constant attention that a mother pays to the face of her child. Damage or abnormality in the fusiform gyrus leads to a condition called "prosopagnosia" or simply "face blindness". Another interesting neural difference between maternal love and romantic love is the hypothalamus, which is involved in sexual arousal, thus only in romantic love.

The influence of Oxytocin and Vasopressin is far more delicate than you can imagine. These two incredible hormones go to great lengths to keep us from being promiscuous. To illustrate this, let me tell you the story of the prairie and the montane voles. It is a story of great biological interest. Among these two species, the prairie voles are mostly monogamous in nature, while the montane voles are promiscuous. Due to their brain circuits, the montane voles cannot maintain a healthy long-term relationship. If the release of Oxytocin and Vasopressin is blocked in prairie voles, they too become promiscuous. If, however, prairie voles are injected with these hormones but prevented from having sex, they will still continue to be faithful to their partners through a chaste monogamous relationship. That makes one wonder, what if we just inject the montane voles with Oxytocin and Vasopressin! Makes sense right!

One might think that injecting the montane voles with these two hormones will somehow magically transform them into faithful monogamous creatures. But quite unfortunately it doesn't work that way. An injection of these "love potions" as I call them, don't render them monogamous. Once secreted by the pituitary, these neurochemicals can only act if there are receptors for them in the brain. In the prairie voles there is an abundance of receptors for Oxytocin and Vasopressin in the reward centers of the brain. While on the contrary in the montane voles, receptors for these two hormones are not as abundant. Ergo, injecting the montane voles with excessive amounts of Oxytocin and Vasopressin doesn't make them monogamous, since there are not sufficient receptors for them in the reward centers.

There is a genetic cause behind this receptor variability. Prairie voles carry a longer version of the vasopressin receptor gene which makes them way more monogamous in behavior than the montane voles. Our two closest primate cousins, chimpanzees and bonobos also have different lengths of this gene, which match their social behaviors especially in the sexual aspect. Chimpanzees, who have the shorter gene, live in territorially based societies controlled by males who make frequent, fatal war raids on neighboring troops. While on the other hand, bonobos are run by female hierarchies and seal every social interaction with a bit of sexual impression. They are exceptionally social and have the long version of the gene.

Bonobos are a uniquely promiscuous species. They live by the code "make love, not war", quite literally. Sex is the key to the social life of the bonobos. Bonobos become sexually aroused remarkably easily, and they express this excitement in a variety of mounting positions and genital contacts. Although chimpanzees virtually never adopt face-to-face positions, bonobos do so in one out of three copulations in the wild. Furthermore, the frontal orientation of the bonobo vulva and clitoris strongly suggest that the female genitalia are adapted for this position.

The most unique sexual behavior in bonobos is genito-genital rubbing between adult females. One female facing another clings with arms and legs to a partner that, standing on both hands and feet, lifts her off the ground. The two females then rub their genital swellings together, emitting grins and squeals that reflect orgasmic experiences.

Figure 2.1 Female bonobos have forward facing genitalia and often have face-to-face sexual contact with other females. Females become sexually mature at 12 years old but will engage in sexual activity from younger ages.

Male bonobos, too, may engage in pseudocopulation but generally perform a variation. Standing back to back, one male briefly rubs his scrotum against the buttocks of another. They also practice "penis-fencing", in which two males hang face to face from a branch while rubbing their erect penises together.

The diversity of erotic contacts in bonobos includes sporadic oral sex, massage of another individual's genitals and intense tongue-kissing. The sexual activity of bonobos is rather casual and relaxed, and appears to be a completely natural part of their group life. Like people, bonobos engage in sex only occasionally, not continuously. Furthermore, with the average copulation lasting 13 seconds, sexual contact in bonobos is rather quick by human standards.

The human version of the vasopressin receptor gene is more like the bonobo gene. Differences in partner commitment may therefore be related to our individual differences in the length of this gene and in hormones. However, unlike bonobos or indeed any other animal, the humans have a well-developed cerebral cortex, which endows us with the typically human faculties of conscience and self-control. It enables us to choose whether or not to act upon the innate primordial urge of promiscuity.

The modern qualities that make us superior to all the animals are intellect and self-control. So, even though it is true that deep within, we are still unconsciously the same old cave-people or simply wild animals craving for sexual satisfaction, we also have developed the neurological capability to keep those instincts in check for a healthier and happier society.

And due to obvious evolutionary reason, men are more primordial in the domain of sexual pursuit. For a man, the optimal evolutionary strategy is to disseminate his genes as widely as possible, given his few minutes or, alas, seconds, of investment in each encounter. While on the contrary, a woman invests a great deal of time and effort - a nine month long, risky, strenuous pregnancy, in each offspring.

Naturally, over the course of millions of years, women have evolved into a more monogamous creature than men, while on the other hand, the tendency of men is to be polygamous and promiscuous. Now the question that may rise in your mind is, if men are biologically more polygamous and women are more monogamous, then how can a romantic relationship ever last for long?

The answer is in the evolution of various brain regions. It is true that men will always be men with their innate wild attraction towards large breasts and big hips around them even while being in a relationship. But through the process of Natural Selection, an amazing brain region evolved inside the skull - the pre-frontal cortex.

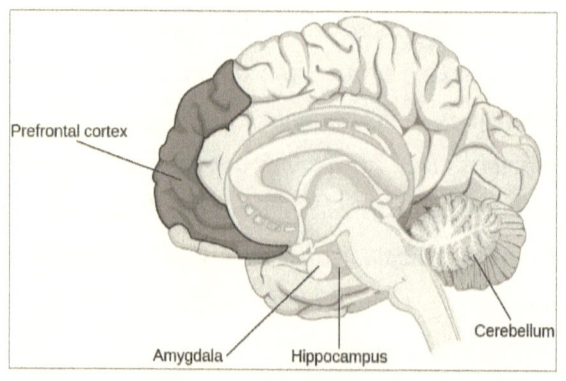

Figure 2.2 Prefrontal Cortex shown as darker region. A healthy prefrontal cortex means better emotional stability.

Prefrontal cortex is the area of the brain that gives you the ability to keep all your momentary emotional impulses in check. It is a small portion in the front part of the cerebral cortex. The entire cerebral cortex is the crowning achievement of primate evolution. It is the constructor of all the your inexplicable and typically human faculties. It is the part of the brain that most distinctively sets us apart from any other species on this planet. And the architect of the cerebral cortex, like all other biological mechanism, is Mother Nature herself.

By putting selective pressure over the hominin brain, Mother Nature made the human brain circuits go through not only quantitative but also qualitative changes, over the period of a few million years. And these changes are most significant in the Cerebral Cortex. In fact, the principles governing the cortical development hold the key to understanding our cognitive capacity of intelligence and creativity.

You must remember, that all your pride of being superior to all other animals on earth, is because of the Cerebral Cortex. Without the highly advanced and complicated neural network of the cortex, there is no difference between us and other animals.

The human cerebral cortex is a laminated structure composed of the most bewildering diversity of neurons arranged in distinct patterns among all the species on earth. We are what we are because of this diversity of neurons in the cerebral cortex. This diversity enables us to become the most advanced as well as civilized species on this planet. However, the human mind also has a neurological predisposition to act in profoundly wild and uncivilized ways. And all our primitive aboriginal urges emerge from this innate predisposition of monstrosity.

This primitive version of our mind lies within the deepest region of the human brain. This region is much more ancient than the modern cerebral cortex of the civilized human mind. It is the Limbic System, that lies right below the layers of the cerebral cortex.

Most of the limbic brain has been there since our reptilian days. The face of this ancient region of the brain is shameless and ill-mannered. It is a wild beast that does not play well with any kind of social norms, unlike the civilized face of the cerebral cortex. These two faces of your mind are completely opposite of each other, yet they work together to keep you up on your feet. It is the fascinating interplay between the Cerebral Cortex and Limbic System, that makes us civilized human beings with heaps of emotions and values.

- ***Love, God & Neurons***

Like all other mental and physical faculties of the human species, the cortical control over emotions evolved out of a growing need to survive in the dreadful environment of the wilderness. It began with our Australopithecine ancestors who lived around three million years ago. They had just left the forest and moved to the savanna where their upright posture helped to see longer distances for scavenging food and watching for predators.

While living in the harsh environment of the wild, a very important tool of survival was being next to each other. This is what we call social organization. And our Australopithecine ancestors had a kind of basic social organization. The freaky surrounding compelled them to live in groups. Once they started to live in groups, they required further social skills in order to manage their social relationship, which in turn proved to be an important trigger for the increase in the brain size. By developing social skills the Australopithecines formed alliances and coalitions within the group in order to supervise their survival inside their society as well as outside of it.

With the limited cranial capacity of about 500 cc, the Australopithecines did indeed encounter the dawn of human consciousness. They developed a kind of emotional communication, which was confined to physical gestures and primitive vocalization. But, such communication system had its own headache. Any negative emotional outbreak could disrupt harmony in the group. Such emotional outbreaks were followed by a lot of noises which attracted attention of the predators. Naturally, this created an adaptive pressure for cortical control of emotions and for the basic social emotions of sympathy, guilt, and shame which promote cohesiveness. This triggered an increase in the brain size which was mostly in the neocortex that added an extra layer to the whole brain and made room for more neurons. In fact, their primitive form of social organization influenced the human brain to embark on an evolutionary journey of becoming the most social, emotional and advanced brain on planet earth.

The limbic system constructs all the emotional elements of your mental universe, which are then imposed on your conscious mind after passing through the cortical gateway of moderation under the watch of the Prefrontal Cortex in the Frontal Lobes of the Cerebral Cortex.

So, even though a man is biologically incapable of ceasing his testosterone level to go high when he visualizes a hot lady, he still can choose whether or not to act upon that momentary impulse of libido, by practicing the healthy functioning of his prefrontal cortex. In fact, if he is in a relationship he can utilize this situation to his best interest, by channeling that momentary surge of lust and slowly shifting the focus on his own partner. Once the body is turned on, it no longer matters whether the satisfaction is coming from the same source that triggered the turn on in the first place. So, it is a fantastic opportunity to add some kink to the relationship.

Sexuality is not just about making love or creating offspring, it is about one's identity. A society that does not recognize sexuality as a natural part of human existence, cannot take a single step in the path of progress. Progress begins only when you start to recognize your true self. Without realizing the self, no great mission can be accomplished. Without the ability to express the self, no life can be truly lived. Liberation lies in the expression of the true self. And if in a society a person does not have the basic freedom to express his or her innate sexuality without the worry of being judged or discriminated, then such a society is more primitive than civilized – such a society is more a kingdom of animals than a world of humans.

3.Homosexuality

Sin, blasphemy, heresy – all these are primitive ideas created by primitive creatures, unworthy of the title "human". These terms have no place in the society of thinking humanity. If any creature advocates for such ideas, then rest assured, it is a mindless ape, not a civilized human. To be called as a human, one has to act like one. In the rapidly disappearing world of these apes, homosexuality falls in the category of sins.

Can you imagine, somebody telling you, your love for your dearly beloved is a sin! Can you imagine, somebody telling you, women are inferior to men, and are meant only serve the men! Can you imagine, somebody telling you, a man can have multiple wives, and yet be deemed civilized! Here that somebody is a fundamentalist ape - a theoretical pest from the stone-age, that somehow managed to survive even amidst all the rise of reasoning and intellect.

Such a creature with no modern mental faculty whatsoever, knows nothing beyond the words of a book, written hundreds or thousands of years ago, when ignorance was the default mode of thinking in the society. It does not only believe every single word of its scripture to be literally true, but puts all its efforts to convince others to believe the same. This way, it would be an understatement to say, such is a worthless creature. In reality, such a creature can cause a catastrophic contagion in a society. However, in this case, the most effective pesticidal effort would be to ignorance its very existence. Such a pest does not even deserve the slightest bit of attention from the civilized and conscientious humans. And lack of attention would eventually incapacitate them from making an impact on the society.

Any human action that goes against what is usual, is deemed as an anomaly, thus earns the title of a "sin". From this perspective, homosexuality can indeed be hailed as an act of sin. But that is all primitive woo-woo stuff. It has nothing to do with the biological reality of life as it is.

However, if you ask for a factual answer on the grounds of empirical evidence, to whether Homosexuality is a sin or not, then, here it is. Homosexuality is neither a sin, nor an anomaly. In biological terms, it is an evolutionary variation. If there is anything related to Homosexuality, that can be termed as a sin from a moral standpoint, it is Homophobia.

Likewise, being a transgender is neither an anomaly nor a disease. It may only be deemed by the ordinary human mind as an anomaly, because it is something out of the ordinary which the mind is usually accustomed to. The same goes for Homosexuals.

Life on earth is really wonderful. It is so vivid and versatile, that one who truly opens his or her eyes can't help being mesmerized by its vivacious beauty. Unaware of that beauty, the primitive society of the so-called humans has long perceived all biological variations as some sort of alien infection. Homosexuality is the most alienated and stigmatized among them.

Despite all our so-called advancements, only recently, people have started to think about the possibility that Homosexuality might not be an anomaly after all. In response to the intellectual vacuum created by the failures of psychiatry to solve the riddle of sexual orientation, we biologists recently embarked on the path of understanding the true biological basis of Homosexuality.

The term itself first appeared in German *"Homosexualität"* in a pamphlet published in Leipzig in 1869; and it entered the English language almost after two decades. During the Middle Ages, engaging in sexual intercourse with a person of the same sex was regarded as a sin. Between the sixteenth and eighteenth century homosexual intercourse became a crime as well as a sin. But things got a little weird in the nineteenth century, when modern medicine and particularly the field of psychiatry (which was more about assumptions than actual science back then), came to view homosexuality as a form of mental illness. It was included in the first Diagnostic and Statistical Manual of the

American Psychiatry Association, published in 1952.

Labeling homosexuality as a form of psychopathology reflected nothing but the psychiatrists' assumptions, derived from longstanding religious, cultural and legal traditions, and their clinical impressions of homosexuals who were seeking psychiatric treatment under the pressure of social norms.

For much of the twentieth century, even the scientific community deemed homosexuality as an aspect of psychopathic, paranoid, and schizoid personality disorders. Hence, the psychiatrists and other doctors of that time, made the "treatment" of homosexuality imperative. The medical profession loathed homosexuality to such an extent that virtually any proposed treatment seemed defensible. Lesbians were forced to submit to hysterectomies and estrogen injections, although it became clear that neither of these had any effect on their sexual orientation. Gay men were subjected to similar monstrosity. We lost many great minds in the hands of those ruthless and blind barbarians.

The most glorious name that comes to my mind is Alan Turing. He was a brilliant mathematician who conceived the modern digital computer. In 1950 he published an article entitled "Computing machinery and intelligence". In this paper he asks the question: *Can machines think?* Unable to define thought (like we are unable to define consciousness) he proposes what he calls an "Imitation game". It is played with three entities, a man (A), a computer (B), and an interrogator (C). The interrogator stays in a room apart. The objective of the game for the interrogator is to determine which of the other two is the man and which is the computer by asking questions. This imitation game is now called the Turing test and certain people believe it can help determine whether a computer is intelligent. No computer till this day has managed to fully fool the interrogator. Such was the genius of Alan Turing.

Yet he faced the most horrifying brutality of the so-called civilized world. He was a homosexual at the time when such an act was a criminal offence in the United Kingdom. Naturally, he was arrested and came to trial on 31 March 1952, after the police learned of his sexual relationship with a young Manchester man. He was convicted and given the choice between imprisonment and hormonal treatment to reduce his libido. Rather than going to prison, he accepted the option of treatment via injections of a synthetic estrogen for the period of one year. This so-called treatment left its scars on Turing, rendering him impotent and caused gynaecomastia (a disorder of the endocrine system in which there is a non-cancerous increase in the size of breast tissue in males). While facing the relentless brutality of mankind, Turing already sensed his impending doom: *"no doubt I shall emerge from it all a different man, but quite who I've not found out."*

On June 8, 1954, Turing was found dead in his house by his housekeeper. He had died the day before of cyanide poisoning, a half-eaten apple beside his bed. The lesson to learn from this dreadful event, is that in the face of human monstrosity, even the brilliant minds become helpless.

In the twentieth century, as psychiatrists made it mandatory to treat homosexuality, doctors tried every possible means, from castration to various kinds of aversion therapy, no matter how vicious. None of these could be shown to change the sexual orientation of a person whatsoever. Because hard as it may sound to the idiotic barbarians, homosexuals are not made, they are born. The shaping of sexual orientation takes place inside the womb during the early period of fetal development. During this time, sexual orientation of a person gets biologically imprinted in the brain circuits never to be erased.

Prenatal sex hormones directly influence the development of the neural network of sexual orientation. Prenatal exposure to an opposite-sex hormonal environment, leads the brain circuits to develop homosexual orientation. This prenatal hormonal environment also has ever-lasting effects on the individual's all kinds of behavioral traits. And once imprinted into the neural map, sexual orientation, as well as all other behavioral traits of a person are absolutely irreversible and indelible.

Now, let me elucidate on how the prenatal hormonal environment leaves an irreversible imprint on a person's sexual orientation.

During the early foetal development, if a genetically female brain is exposed to higher levels of testosterone, a male sex hormone, it leads the entire nervous system including the brain circuits to develop along more male-typical lines. While on the other hand, if a genetically male brain is exposed to higher estrogen, a female sex hormone, it leads the entire nervous system including the brain circuits to develop along more female-typical lines.

The complex and fascinating wirings of the human brain for sexual orientation occur during fetal development, following the blueprint of that individual's genes and sex hormones. The behavioral expression of his or her brain wiring will then be influenced and shaped by environment and culture. Thus, environmental and social norms can influence a person's identity, but they cannot alter something so rudimentary – the biological blueprint of sexual orientation.

The biological manifestation of sexual blueprint can be observed in different brain structures of men and women. Take the anterior commissure for example. It is the bundle of high-speed fibers, that connects the two hemispheres of the brain. The functional aspect of this structure is that it is involved in various brain processes related to cognitive abilities and language. In straight women, it is anatomically larger than in straight men. Such sexual dimorphism gives straight women better cognitive abilities and verbal fluency than straight men.

But things get interesting when it comes to homosexual brain. The sexual dimorphism of anterior commissure seen in heterosexual brains, is reversed in homosexual brains. Hence, between a homosexual man and woman, it is the man that has better cognitive abilities and verbal fluency than the homosexual woman. Also we can say that a gay man has better verbal fluency than a straight man, and a straight woman has better verbal fluency than a lesbian.

Another fascinating anatomical difference between the homosexual brain and heterosexual brain, lies in the connectivity of amygdala, the fear response center of the brain. Brain scan studies have shown that the connectivity of the amygdala in the gay male brain is more like that of the straight female brain than of the straight male brain. Whereas, in the lesbian brain it is more like that of the straight male brain than of the straight female brain.

The sexually dimorphic wirings of amygdala lead to better startle response in straight women, than straight men. But, in case of homosexual wirings of the amygdala, the story is exactly the opposite. Lesbians have a lower startle response than straight women, but in a similar range to straight men. Whereas, gay men have more startle response than straight men, in a similar range to straight women.

All these studies are eloquent proof that homosexuality has nothing to do with pathology, but it has all to do with biology.

Biologically speaking, prenatal opposite-sex hormonal exposure and genetic variation lead to homosexual traits. It is simply a biological variation of human sexual behavior. Therefore, it is not an anomaly or a disease.

We the neuroscientists have spent decades trying to understand the phenomenon of sexual orientation and the biological functions underneath it. It is really a fundamental concept that must not be taken lightly. All our countless experiments, observations and examinations of the human biology, lead to one simple conclusion:

Homosexuality is not an abnormality, it is a variation.

And it is not just in the world of humans that we get to observe same sex orientation. Homosexuality is also observed distinctly throughout the animal kingdom. The phenomenon has been reported in more than 1500 animal species, and is well documented for 500 of them, but the real extent is probably much higher.

The variety and ubiquity of same-sex sexual behavior in animals is impressive. Many thousands of instances of same-sex courtship, pair bonding and copulation have been observed in a wide range of species, including mammals, birds, reptiles, amphibians, insects, mollusks and nematodes. These observations are likely to be underestimates of the frequency of such interactions, partly because researchers assume that pairs in sexually monomorphic species that are engaging in sexual behavior must be opposite sexes.

Let me give you a few examples of same-sex sexual behavior in the animal kingdom. I have already mentioned the Bonobos in the previous chapter, now let's look at some other animals that exhibit homosexual behavior.

Bottlenose dolphins show one of the highest rates of same-sex sexual behavior documented in any animal. Male–male mounting, genital contact and "goosing" appear to strengthen alliances between small groups of males and provide practice for later opposite-sex encounters. Female– female sexual behavior also occurs, but to a much lesser extent.

Penguins in captivity can form long-lasting same-sex pair bonds and engage in same-sex sexual behaviors, including copulation.

Some male Garter snakes mimic females in size or pheromone attributes, and are courted by other males when females are absent. However, male–male courtship is not likely a result of mistaken sex recognition. Attracting male courtship might allow solitary males to thermoregulate and protect themselves.

Figure 3.1 A male lion mounting another male

Laysan albatross in Hawaiian populations form long-term female–female pair bonds, which include courtship displays, copulation, mutual grooming behavior and egg incubation.

Even in the animal kingdom, Homosexuality is not just about casual sex, rather it is also about lasting relationship between two females or two males, such as in the bottlenose dolphins.

However, the most intriguing feature of Homosexual behavior is that it is in no way different than heterosexual behavior in terms of psychological dynamics as well as parental ability. Let's take humans for example. The psychological dynamics of heterosexual and homosexual relationships are just the same regardless of what you hear from the stupid and superstitious part of the population. Which means, there is no difference in the true sensation of love between a heterosexual couple and a homosexual couple. The psychological adjustments made by the partners are just the same in both heterosexual and homosexual relationships. Even in terms of duration of the relationship, same-sex partners stay together for 20 years or even longer, just like heterosexual partners.

And as for parental capabilities, despite the baseless claims of those who oppose gay parents, no empirical study shows that having a gay male or lesbian parent is deleterious to children. Consequently, a growing number of courts have finally started to regard sexual orientation as irrelevant to a parent's ability to provide a good and healthy upbringing for his or her children.

In the 1990s, an unprecedented number of homosexual women and men chose to become parents in committed homosexual relationships. Many homosexual men and women had been parents before this time, but their children were usually conceived in a heterosexual marriage. Homosexual parents have often faced hostility from the conservative and apparently blind parts of the society, and have even been denied custody of their own children in many cases. If this is what we call civilization, then I am afraid we are no more civilized than the bonobos. Discriminations are never a sign of a civilized society. What makes us civilized is our act of liberated kindness with other people beyond the man-made primitive citadels of gender, race, religion and sexual orientation.

Sexual orientation defines only sexual orientation, nothing else. It does not define a person's mental capacities. It does not define a person's passions. And above all, it does not define a person's character.

In 1956, Chicago, a young psychologist named Evelyn Hooker (yes, that was her name) presented a study to a meeting of the American Psychological Association. She herself during her training routinely studied the so-called theory of homosexuality as a pathology. A group of young gay men with whom she had become friendly seemed, however, to be quite healthy and lucid in all daily activities. It suddenly appeared to Hooker that the scientific community still didn't know about Homosexuality. So, she received a study grant from the National Institute of Mental Health and chose a group of thirty gay men as the objects of her research and thirty straight men as controls. None of the sixty had ever sought or undergone psychiatric treatment. It was the first time that homosexuals had been studied outside a medical setting or prison.

She conducted psychological tests on her sixty subjects, including the Rorschach ink-blot test, producing sixty psychological profiles. She removed all identifying marks, including those indicating sexual orientation. In order to eliminate her own biases, she gave them for interpretation to three eminent psychologists. One of them was Bruno Klopfer, who believed that he would be able to distinguish homosexuals from heterosexuals by means of the Rorschach test. However, quite astonishingly, none of the three could differentiate the homosexuals from the heterosexuals. In side-by-side comparisons of matched profiles, the heterosexuals and homosexuals were indistinguishable, demonstrating an equal distribution of pathology and mental health.

Hence, Hooker concluded from the study that homosexuality did not constitute a clinical entity and that it was not associated with pathology whatsoever. Her research was driven by her strong then-unconventional belief that for psychiatry to be minimally scientific, pathology must be defined in a way that is objective and empirically observable. Her findings were subsequently replicated in numerous empirical studies of both women and men. The weight of growing empirical evidence, coupled with changing social norms and the development of politically active gay community in the United States of America, compelled the Directors of the American Psychiatric Association to officially remove homosexuality from the Diagnostic and Statistical Manual, in 1973.

The movement to declassify homosexuality as a diagnosis has been strongly supported by the American Psychological Association (APA.) ever since 1974. APA has passed numerous legal resolutions to support equal right for lesbians and gay men in employment, child custody and access to services.

However, there is still a huge difference between theory and practice. Humans shall always remain humans, no matter the position of science. Ever since 1973, the scientific approach among the mainstream psychotherapists has been to help the homosexual clients adjust successfully to their sexual orientation and live life to the fullest. Despite all this, some (non-)psychotherapists and religious counselors continue to make disgraceful attempts to convert homosexuals into heterosexuals.

Regardless of all this, after conducting relentless neurobiological studies, on the biological foundation of sexual orientation, we have been able to move Homosexuality from the domain of psychiatric illnesses into the realm of normal variants of human sexual behavior. And the resulting fact of such an accomplishment is this:

Homosexuality is immutable, irreversible and nonpathological.

A particular sexual orientation is no way an indication of either good or evil. It is not the gender of the two individuals in a relationship that matters, but the content of that relationship. Is there violence in the relationship? Is there enslavement of one partner by the other? Is the relationship a healthy place for the growth of both partners involved? These should be the standards with which relationships all sexual orientations should be measured. And those who think homosexuality is abnormal, to them I say, being homosexual is no more abnormal than being lefthanded. And since we are talking about abnormalities and sins, let me add one more factual revelation for the fundamentalist idiots. It is that, masturbating is no more sinful than praying or meditating.

In fact, masturbation and meditation both promote physical and mental wellbeing. In the most ancient myths of Mesopotamia and Egypt, the god Apsu, or Atun, "copulated with his fist" to fertilize himself and create either the Milky Way or the atmosphere, depending on what version is being told. Masturbation was common among Greek women and men. Although the ancient Spartans' rigid code of self-discipline discouraged masturbation, the Greeks saw it as a gift from the gods. They believed that the god Hermes taught his son Pan how to masturbate to relieve himself of the misery he felt when he was spurned by the nymph, Echo. Pan learned the lesson well, overcame his grief, and taught the trick to human shepherds.

Divinely inspired or not, masturbation was considered a private activity. When the philosopher Diogenes masturbated in public in the agora, he shocked people. He tried to make the point that all human activities are worthy of being done in public - that none of them is so shameful that it requires privacy. His fellow citizens disagreed however.

Women in ancient Athens commonly purchased dildos - olisbos. These fake penises, exported from the city of Miletus in Asia Minor and made of padded leather or wood, were used for masturbation. In Aristophanes' play, Lysistrata, the women who are on a sex strike to force their men to end the Peloponnesian War make jokes about using dildos. Masturbation by adult Greek men was thought of as a sign of poverty. Men who had money would pay a sex worker instead. A few centuries later, Roman boys were expected to channel their sexual energies through gymnastics and philosophy, and to avoid masturbation because it would cause them to mature too rapidly.

Early in the modern era, misguided Swiss physician Samuel August Tissot recapitulated the horrors of masturbation in his 1760 publication, "L'Onanisme, ou Dissertation Physique sur les Maladies Produites par la Masturbation", which, through its hundreds of editions, variations, and imitators — from Voltaire to Rousseau to Immanuel Kant to signatories of the American Declaration of Independence — promulgated the mythology of the evils of masturbation and the so-called "post-masturbation disease" throughout Europe and America. Tissot's admonishments about masturbation were published well into the 20th century and created a worldwide fear of masturbation that continues to cause pain for young and old alike. In Onanisme, Tissot offered "treatment by terror," as exemplified in this cautionary tale about a man he allegedly treated for post-masturbation disease:

I went to his home; what I found was less a living being than a cadaver lying on straw, thin, pale, exuding a loathsome stench, almost incapable of movement. A pale and watery blood often dripped from his nose, he drooled continually; subject to attacks of diarrhea, he defecated in his bed without noticing it; there was constant flow of semen; his eyes, sticky, blurry, dull, had lost all power of movement; his pulse was extremely weak and racing; labored respiration, extreme emaciation, except for the feet, which were showing signs of edema. Mental disorder was equally evident; without ideas, without memory, incapable of linking two sentences, without reflection, without fear of his fate, lacking all feeling except that of pain, which returned at least every three days with each new attack. Thus sunk below the level of the beast, a spectacle of unimaginable horror, it was difficult to believe that he had once belonged to the human race. . . . He died after several weeks, in June 1757, his entire body covered in edemas.

The troubles experienced by women are just as explicable as those experienced by men. The humor they lose being less precious, less perfected than male sperm, its loss does not perhaps weaken them as quickly; but when they indulge excessively, their nervous system being weaker and naturally more inclined to spasm, the troubles are more violent

Tissot claimed also that the self-loathing experienced by masturbators would often lead to suicide. Tissot's work was widely read and generally accepted. Originally written in French, it was translated into several languages, including English, and went through 80 editions. In these editions, Tissot claimed that the ills resulting from masturbation included poor eyesight, epilepsy, memory loss, pulmonary tuberculosis, rounded shoulders, weakened backs, paleness, acne, gonorrhea, and syphilis.

To cure the "state of degeneracy''' supposedly caused by masturbation, American physician and co-signer of the Declaration of Independence, Benjamin Rush, suggested "a vegetable diet, temperance, bodily labor, cold baths, avoidance of obscenity, music, a close study of mathematics, military glory, and, if all else failed, castor oil."

Physicians involved in the social hygiene movement of the 19th and early 20th centuries continued to diagnose and treat conditions thought to be sequelae of masturbation. Cures varied from concocted food products and diets designed specifically to decrease sexual drive to techniques and devices used to prevent sexual arousal and masturbation. For example, Sylvester Graham invented his famous crackers as part of a diet of whole grains and vegetables designed to decrease sexual desire.

In his book, Plain Facts (1888), J.H. Kellogg, M.D., cautioned readers that masturbating was the most dangerous of sexual behaviors. According to Kellogg, the causes of masturbation included idleness, abnormal sexual passions, gluttony, sedentary employment, and exciting and irritating food. Kellogg's recommendations for preventing masturbation in children included serving cold instead of hot cereals for breakfast, bandaging their genitals, and/or tying their hands to the bedposts at night.

At the turn of the century, a number of other techniques were used to keep children's hands away from their sex organs. These included confinement in straitjackets or wrappings of cold, wet sheets while sleeping, applying leeches onto the genitals to remove blood and congestion allegedly created by desire, burning genital tissue with electric current or a hot iron, castration, and removing the clitoris. Anti-masturbation contraptions included *"a genital cage that used springs to hold a boy's penis and scrotum in place and a device that sounded an alarm if a boy had an erection"*, metal mittens for covering children's hands, rings of metal spikes meant to stab the penis if it became erect, and metal vulva guards.

To reduce female masturbation, Isaac Baker, an English physician, performed clitoridectomies. In the U.S., physicians advocated and performed male circumcision to prevent masturbation in male infants. In fact, the American tradition of circumcision is based on the fear of sexual arousal and subsequent masturbation resulting from the stimulation a boy might allegedly experience while cleaning his uncircumcised penis.

In the 19th and early 20th centuries, parents were encouraged to prevent their children from masturbating with the following techniques.

• They could take their children to a wax museum where the effects of post-masturbation disease were displayed with life-size, grotesquely deformed statuettes, or they could show their children engravings of a woman who lost her nose by masturbating.

• They could make sure their children had at least two bouts of strenuous gymnastic exercise every day so that they would fall asleep at night without having enough energy to masturbate. But parents should not allow their children the sport of horseback riding, especially galloping, until their characters were more perfectly developed. Boxing and other exercise of the upper body were especially recommended.

• They could see to it that their children swam every day or had cold baths or showers. It was believed that preventing a buildup of sweat on the skin would reduce the kinds of bodily irritations that led to masturbating.

• They could keep their children away from "heat-producing" environments, such as feather beds.

• They could make their children wear bathing suits with bags of camphor inserted in the crotch.

• They could keep an eye on the children's diets. Children were to avoid hot or "exciting" foods: spices, rich meats, venison, salted fish, and wine. They were to avoid constipation, which could bring on the desire to masturbate. They were to have simple, nutritious foods: grains, milk, cheese, bread.

• They could limit the amount of fluid their children took in because *"abundant urine retained too long in the bladder . . . draws too much blood to the very part from which we want to draw it away"*.

• They could insist that their sons refrain from shaking their penises after urinating, even it meant dripping a little urine in their pants.

• They could, like many other parents, tie their children's hands to the bed rails at night.

• They could buy chastity belts, garments (e.g., hand mufflers and straitjackets), and devices into which they could strap their children to prevent them from being able to reach or touch their genitals, or they could purchase toothed urethral rings that would prick the penis if it became erect, metal strap-on-and-lock sheaths to cover the penis or vulva, or electric alarms that promised to put an end to wet dreams.

• They could be sure that their children's teachers furnished their classrooms with anti-masturbation school benches, forcing boys to keep their legs apart. *"Thus both the rubbing and the heating of the genital parts are avoided,"* eliminating one of the causes of masturbation. Preferred classroom furniture did not allow the lower part of a student's body to be hidden from the teacher's view. Likewise, long coats were to be avoided by students.

• They could fatigue their children with medicinal teas: orange flowers, centaury, violets, marshmallow, couch grass, purslane, lettuce, and lily.

• They could terrify their children into abstinence by brandishing knives, scissors, or surgical instruments at them with threats to cut off their genitals.

• They could have the foreskin of their child's penis infibulated — pierced, then pulled beyond the glans, and closed shut with an iron ring.

• They could have the hood of their child's clitoris infibulated — have the child's labia stitched together with metal sutures. Or they could have the clitoris amputated.

• They could have the urethra of the child repeatedly cauterized so that it would always be painful and unpleasant to touch.

• They could have a doctor apply caustic chemicals such as potassium bromide to the child's clitoris or penis. The pain and tissue destruction were intended to terrorize children out of their masturbatory habits.

• They could marry their children off, because marriage was the ultimate and most effective preventive. It was the method that King Leopold I of Belgium intended to use with his oldest son as he explained in an 1853 letter to Queen Victoria.

Circumcision was first suggested as a cure for masturbation in boys in 1885 by Charles K. Mills. He also wrote "A Case of Nymphomania with Hysterio-Epilepsy and Peculiar Mental Perversions — the Results of Clitirodectomy and Oophorectomy — The Patient's History as Told by Herself," an article published in the Philadelphia Medical Times.

It was not until the last year of the 19th century, that a leading authority in Philadelphia finally spoke out against the social hysteria regarding masturbation. In 1899, the pioneer British sexologist, Havelock Ellis, fearful of censorship in England, published the second part of the first volume of "Studies in the Psychology of Sex: The Evolution of Modesty, the Phenomena of Sexual Periodicity, & Auto-Eroticism". In it, Ellis confronted Tissot and his followers. He said they were responsible for:

> *the mistaken notions of many medical authorities, carried on by tradition, even down to our own time; the powerful lever which has been put into the hand of unscrupulous quacks; the suffering, dread, and remorse experienced in silence by many thousands of ignorant and often innocent young people . . . During the past forty years the efforts of many distinguished physicians . . . have gradually dragged the bogy down from its pedestal, and now . . . there is even a tendency today to regard masturbation as normal.*

Despite all the primitively constructed stigmas attached to the very idea of masturbation its practice has most gloriously survived through time. That is because it is a natural, and more importantly, healthy practice of a functional body.

In the late 1940s and early 1950s, Alfred Kinsey and his colleagues published the results of more than 15 years' worth of research in human sexual behavior. One of the most important results of that work was the normalization of masturbation and the weakening of the stigma against it. Kinsey's research revealed that more people had masturbated than had not. Between 92 and 97 percent of the men in his 1948 study, "Sexual Behavior in the Human Male", had masturbated (Kinsey, et al., 1948, 339). And 62 percent of the women in his 1953 study, Sexual Behavior in the Human Female, had masturbated — 58 percent of them had masturbated to orgasm. Although masturbation was the second most frequently practiced sexual behavior among women, married or single, it was the behavior in which orgasm was most frequently achieved (Kinsey, et al., 1953, 142– 4).

Kinsey also revealed details about the masturbation techniques of women: *84 percent of women stroked or stimulated the inner lips and/or clitoris, and 10 percent crossed their legs and exerted a steady rhythmic pressure affecting the whole area. Others employed vibrators or rubbed against pillows, beds, tables, and other objects. Two percent could orgasm from fantasy. Twenty percent of women used penetration during masturbation in conjunction with other methods* (Kinsey, et al., 189). While the American public had been able to accept Kinsey's earlier report on the sexual activities of men, it could not accept his description of the sexual behaviors of American women — masturbating, having orgasms, pre-marital sex, extra-marital sex, or sex with each other. All over the country, churches rose in protest.

For example, without reading Kinsey's work, Billy Graham wrote, *"It is impossible to estimate the damage this book will do to the already deteriorating morals of America,"* and Senator Joe McCarthy denounced Kinsey's work as part of the Communist conspiracy. All over America, people named Kinsey took out newspaper ads saying they were not related to him. Ultimately, as a result of the furor, the Rockefeller Foundation withdrew its support for Kinsey's research.

Studies after Kinsey's death continued to corroborate his findings. In 1969, for example, German researchers asked men to masturbate every few hours over a period of two years — no evidence of either physical or mental disease or disorder was detected. By 1975, a study of U.S. college students revealed that 84 percent did not believe that masturbation caused emotional or mental instability — a total reversal of attitudes that prevailed in U.S. colleges in 1937.

In 1968 and 1969, Kinsey's colleague, Wardell Pomeroy, wrote "Boys and Sex" and "Girls and Sex". In them, he advised children about masturbation, and reassured girls and boys that *"no physical harm can come of it, contrary to the old beliefs, no matter how frequently it is done."* In fact, Pomeroy said that masturbation was *"a pleasurable and exciting experience. . . . It releases tensions, and is therefore valuable in many ways. . . . It provides a full outlet for fancy, for daydreaming, which is characteristic of adolescence. . . . In itself, it offers a variety that enriches the individual's sex life. . . . it is not only harmless but is positively good and healthy, and should be encouraged because it helps young people to grow up sexually in a natural way"* (Pomeroy, 1968, 48–58). Finally, the American medical community pronounced masturbation as normal in the 1972 American Medical Association publication, "Human Sexuality".

Now let's take a look at the effects of meditation on life and biology. In this context, let me bring up an excerpt from my book "Rowdy Buddha: The First Sapiens".

Meditation makes your mind go through diverse biological mechanisms, which in turn have profound impact upon all aspects of life, especially your mental life. The very first stage is activation of your frontal lobes, as you begin focusing your attention on an object, breathing, chant, or an imaginary bright light between the eyebrows.

During the process, the activation of your brain's attention area - prefrontal cortex (in frontal lobes), starts inhibiting various other brain activities, through the hippocampus, except the ones that generate a kind of ecstatic bliss. Then the brain region that enables your conscious spatial-temporal orientation, i.e. the parietal lobe starts to become less active. And eventually, over a long period of practice, ten to twenty minutes every day, you lose not only your sense of self, but also your sense of space and time, as the parietal lobes shut down almost completely.

Also, the limbic system, which is the house of all your emotions, is highly involved in meditation activities. The involvement of this region leads to a feeling of arousal and ecstasy during the practice, even in the early days.

Over the last few decades, with the amazing advancement of brain imaging techniques, we the neuroscientists have been endowed with the ability to take a closer look at brain functions during various tasks. With the use of single-photon emission computed tomography

(SPECT) scans, we now can capture the actual brain state of an individual engaged in secular, religious or spiritual rituals such as meditation or prayer.

This SPECT technology is really fascinating. To, know what kind of alterations in brain functions take place when you meditate or pray (prayer is essentially a kind of meditation), a harmless, radioactive tracer is injected at the time of the practice. The tracer gets locked into the brain, and it shows exactly what's going on in the brain at the moment of the practice.

Then, we can look at the brain scans and compare the resting state (when the person isn't doing anything in particular) to the activation state (the state when the person is actually engaged in the practice of meditation or prayer) in order to see what areas of the brain are turned on or off. With SPECT scans, we scientists also have the ability to apply a quantitative analysis of the meditation or prayer state of your brain. We can tell how much, in terms of percentages, a part of your brain is active or inactive while you are engaged in meditation or prayer.

Apart from the attainment of Nirvana, when you embrace meditation in your daily life, you inadvertently embark on an ever-positive journey towards better health, both physiological and psychological. The practice of meditation results in decreased heart rate, blood pressure, metabolism and hormonal changes. Also, it results in increased level of serotonin, dopamine, and gamma-aminobutyric acid (GABA), which are the body's natural anti-anxiety drugs, and decreased level of the stress hormone cortisol. At the very least, long-term practice of meditation leads to emotional stability and endows you with a sense of calmness even in stressful situations of modern life.

- *Rowdy Buddha: The First Sapiens*

So you see, the ideas that primitive humans hailed abnormal and sinful were all founded upon ignorance, superstition and barbarianism. Barbarianism paved the way for Homophobia. And I am pain-stricken to say that it still shamelessly prevails in various parts of the so-called human society, mostly in the name of religion. The homophobes delude themselves with the notion that babbling some biblical passage like a mindless parrot makes them religious. In reality, the true religion is nowhere near it. True religion comes not from a book, but it rises from the heart of a conscientious human. True religion is the realization of the self. There is nothing else. There is nothing higher.

You are modern humans of the civilized world. And modern humans rise beyond all laws and superstitions of the society. They help their fellow beings to rise from the ashes of ignorance, illusion and fear. The salvation of society, therefore, depends on the strength of the individual, beyond the discriminations of gender, race and sexual identity. It depends on you. It depends on your realization of the self. It depends of your realization of your true identity.

Morality does not come to this mortal world from some imaginary paradise. It rises from the neurons of mortal humans to aid in the process of a healthy conduct in both personal and social life of the mortal humans. Hence, it is the existential responsibility of the humans to reconstruct the moral parameters of a time based on the advancements and achievements of that time. It is your responsibility my friend, to contribute to the reconstruction of the moral parameters of your society. You, my friend, are endowed with the existential responsibility to shape your society towards a world free from prejudices and discriminations.

Discriminations suit animals, not humans. And yet, the unfortunate reality is, it is the humans that discriminate each other on the grounds of imaginary labels, not the animals. This way, animals are more civilized than humans.

Forget race, forget gender, forget religion, and become a human my friend. Become a human above everything else, and all great things shall follow. Become a human and call upon the humans in others. And in time the world shall become a real abode of peace. Take a pledge with me today. Speak up with me – *"I - a conscientious human of the civilized world - pledge that I shall leave a better, healthier and more loving society for my children than the one I received from my ancestors."*

Do your part my friend, and forget about the outcome. Do your part, and at the very least, you will die knowing that you did your best. It is a billion times more glorious to die while doing your part for the wellbeing and progress of the society than to live a long life under the oppression of the primordial norms of an idiotic and barbarian society. Start working my friend – start working towards humanizing the world. Because the world needs humans – conscientious humans, not some dumb manikins, driven by prejudice and discrimination. Humanize the world my friend. Humanize the world, even if it means sacrificing everything that you have – even if it means going against the very people that you hold dear.

Bring your rational thinking into practice and scrutinize every single norm of the society with critical reasoning. The truth shall always pass the test of human reasoning no matter how critical you become of it. But it is the lies and prejudices that shall get terminated in the process. Remember this, truth welcomes rational criticism, whereas prejudices demand irrefutable obedience. And in world of civilized humans it is the faculty of conscience that must prevail, not obedience of any sort.

Believe in something, not because some ancient text says so, not because your forefathers command you thus, not because your society demands from you such, but because you can think for yourself. Seek the truth with all the powers that are hidden within you. Stop being the sheep and become the lion my friend! Sheeps can't find the truth. Sheeps can't be free from prejudices. Sheeps can't build a civilized and progressive society. It is the lion that can do that. It is better to be a lion for a day than to be a sheep for a whole life.

You are the heir of infinite strength my friend! Recognize that strength and throw away all the prejudices that your society has been imposing upon you since birth. Widen your mind and make it crystal clear – and once you do, you will become a true human being – a human being in whose veins would run purity and conscience – a human being whose nerves would be made of courage – a human being whose heart would beat with the rhythm of humanism.

BIBLIOGRAPHY

Anchell, Melvin. (1991). "What's Wrong With Sex Education?": Preteen and Teenage Sexual Development and Environmental Influences. Portland, OR: Halcyon House.

Acevedo BP, Aron A, Fisher HE & Brown LL (2011). Neural correlates of long-term intense romantic love. Social Cognitive and Affective Neuroscience, published online January 5 2011.

Aron A (2006). Relationship neuroscience: Advancing the social psychology of close relationships using functional neuroimaging. In PAM Van Lange (Ed) Bridging social psychology: Benefits of transdisciplinary approaches, Lawrence Erlbaum Associates Publishers Mahwah NJ.

Aron A (2010). Behavior the brain and the social psychology of close relationships. In CR Agnew, DE Carlston, WG Graziano & JR Kelly (Eds) Then a miracle occurs: Focusing on behavior in social psychological theory and research, Oxford University Press New York.

Aron A, Fisher H, Mashek DJ, Strong G, Li H & Brown LL (2005). Reward motivation and emotion systems associated with early-stage intense romantic love. Journal of Neurophysiology 94.

Aron AP & Aron EN (1986). Love as the expansion of self: Understanding attraction and satisfaction. Hemisphere, New York.

Aron AP & Aron EN (1991). Love and sexuality. In K McKinney & S Sprecher (Eds.) Sexuality in close relationship. Lawrence Erlbaum Associates, Hillsdale, NJ.

Aristophanes (trans. Charles T. Murphy). (1957) Lysistrata. In L.R. Lind, editor, Ten Greek Plays in Contemporary Translations. Boston: Houghton Mifflin Company.

Benson, H., and M. Z. Klipper. The Relaxation Response. New York: Harper Torch, 1976.

Blessing, B., and I. Gibbons. "Autonomic Nervous System." Scholarpedia 3, no.7 (2008)

Bourne, E. J. The Anxiety and Phobia Workbook. 3rd ed. San Francisco, CA: New Harbinger Press, 2000.

Breedlove, S. M., N. V. Watson, and M. R. Rosenzsweig. Biological Psychology: An Introduction to Behavioral, Cognitive, and Clinical Neuroscience. 6th ed. Sunderland, MA: Sinauer Associates Press, 2005.

Bronfenbrenner, U. The Ecology of Human Development: Experiments by Nature and Design. Cambridge, MA: Harvard University Press, 1979.

Brooks, D. The Social Animal: The Hidden Sources of Love, Character, and Achievement. New York: Random House, 2011.

Brownell, K. D., R. Kersh, D. D. Ludwig, R. C. Post, R. M. Puhl, M. B. Schwartz, and W. C. Willett. "Personal Responsibility and Obesity: A Constructive Approach to a Controversial Issue." Health Affairs 29, no. 3 (March 2010)

Burns, D. D. Feeling Good: The New Mood Therapy. New York: Signet, 1980.

Babayev ES, Allahverdiyeva AA. Effects of geomagnetic activity variations on the physiological and psychological state of functionally healthy humans: some results of Azerbaijani studies. Adv Space Res 2007.

Baars, B. (1988), A Cognitive Theory of Consciousness (New York: Cambridge University Press).

Bartels A & Zeki S (2000). The neural basis of romantic love. Neuroreport:

For Rapid Communication of Neuroscience Research 11.

Bartels A & Zeki S (2004). The neural correlates of maternal and romantic love. Neuroimage 21.

Basson R (2000). The female sexual response: A different model. Journal of Sex & Marital Therapy 26, 51-65.

Basson R (2002). Women's sexual desire: Disordered or misunderstood? Journal of Sex & Marital Therapy 28.

Basson R, Wierman ME, van Lankveld J & Brotto L (2010). Summary of the recommendations on sexual dysfunctions in women. Journal of Sexual Medicine 7.

Baumeister RF (2000). Gender differences in erotic plasticity: The female sex drive as socially flexible and responsive. Psychological Bulletin 126.

Beauregard M, Courtemanche J, Paquette V & St-Pierre EL (2009). The neural basis of unconditional love. Psychiatry Research: Neuroimaging 172.

Bianchi-Demicheli F, Grafton ST & Ortigue S (2006). The power of love on the human brain. Social Neuroscience 1.

Bocher M, Chisin R, Parag Y, Freedman N, Meir Weil Y, Lester H et al. (2001). Cerebral activation associated with sexual arousal in response to a pornographic clip: A 15O-H2O PET study in heterosexual men. Neuroimage 14.

Bagemihl, Bruce. (1999). Biological Exuberance: Animal Homosexuality and Natural Diversity. New York: St. Martin's Press.

Berne, Eric. (1944). "The Problem of Masturbation." Diseases of the Nervous System, 5(10), 301–305.

Blundell, Sue. (1995). Women in Ancient Greece. Cambridge, Massachessetts: Harvard University Press.

Brashear, Diane B. (1974). "Honk! If You Masturbate!" Siecus Report III, 2 (1), 4.

Bullough, Vern L. (1994). Science in the Bedroom — A History of Sex Research. New York: BasicBooks.

Bullough, Vern L. & Bonnie Bullough. (1995). Sexual Attitudes: Myths and Realities. New York: Prometheus Books.

Brotto LA, Bitzer J, Laan E, Leiblum SR & Luria M (2010). Women's sexual desire and arousal disorders. Journal of Sexual Medicine 7.

Boyer, Pascal. Religion Explained. New York: Basic Books, 2002

Buss, D. D. (2003). Evolutionary Psychology: The New Science of Mind,

2nd ed. New York: Allyn &Bacon. Buss, D. M. (1989). "Conflict between the sexes: Strategic interference and the evocation of anger and upset." J Pers Soc Psychol 56 (5).

Buss, D. M. (1995). "Psychological sex differences. Origins through sexual selection." Am Psychol 50 (3).

Buss, D. M. (2002). "Review: Human Mate Guarding." Neuro Endocrinol Lett 23 (Suppl 4).

Buss, D. M., and D. P. Schmitt (1993). "Sexual strategies theory: An evolutionary perspective on human mating." Psychol Rev 100 (2).

Carter CS (1998). Neuroendocrine perspectives on social attachment and love. Psychoneuroendocrinology 23.

Carter CS & Keverne EB (2002). The neurobiology of social affiliation and pair bonding. In J Pfaff AP Arnold AE Etgen & SE Fahrbach (Eds) Hormones brain and behavior, vol. 1. Academic Press, New York.

Campbell A. The limbic system and emotion in relation to acupuncture. Acupuncture in Medicine.1999.

Cowan CP, Cowan PA. When Partners Become Parents: The Big Life Change for Couples. New York: Basic Books; 1992.

Chivers ML & Bailey JM (2005). A sex difference in features that elicit genital response. Biological Psychology 70.

Chivers ML, Rieger G, Latty E & Bailey JM (2004). A sex difference in the specificity of sexual arousal. Psychological Science 15.

Chivers ML Seto MC & Blanchard R (2007). Gender and sexual orientation differences in sexual response to sexual activities versus gender of actors in sexual films. Journal of Personality and Social Psychology 93.

Calderone, Mary S. & Eric W. Johnson. (1981). The Family Book About Sexuality. New York: Harper & Row.

Carter, Julian B. (2001). "Birds, Bees, and Vernereal Disease: Toward an Intellectual History of Sex Education." Journal of the History of Sexuality, 10(2), 213–249.

Christensen, Clark. (1995). "Prescribed Masturbation in Sex Therapy: A Critique." Journal of Sex & Marital Therapy, 21(2), 87–99.

Crooks, Robert and Karla Baur. (1983). "Sexual Behavior Patterns." In Our Sexuality. Menlo Park, CA: The Benjamin/Cummings Publishing Company.

Dixson, Barnaby J. and Brookes, Robert C. "The role of facial hair in women's perceptions of men's attractiveness, health, masculinity and parenting abilities" Evolution and Human Behavior 34, 2013

Diamond LM (2003). What does sexual orientation orient? A biobehavioral model distinguishing romantic love and sexual desire. Psychological Review 110.

Diamond LM (2005). From the heart or the gut? Sexual-minority women's experiences of desire for same-sex and other-sex partners. Feminism and Psychology 15

Diamond LM (2008). Sexual fluidity: Understanding women's love and desire. Harvard University Press, Cambridge, MA.

Diamond LM & Wallen K (2011). Sexual-minority women's sexual motivation around the time of ovulation. Archives of Sexual Behavior 40

Davidson, J. Kenneth, and Nelwyn. B. Moore. (1994). "Masturbation and Premarital Sexual Intercourse Among College Women: Making Choices for

Sexual Fulfillment." Journal of Sex and Marital Therapy, 20(3), 178–199.

Dodson, Betty. (1996). Sex for One. New York: Three Rivers Press.

Dover, K.J. (1989). Greek Homosexuality. Cambridge, MA: Harvard University Press.

Esch, T. and Stefano, G.B "The Neurobiology of Love" Neuroendocrinology Letters No.3 June Vol.26, 2005.

Ferretti A, Caulo M, Del Gratta C, Di Matteo R, Merla A, Montorsi F et al. (2005). Dynamics of male sexual arousal: distinct components of brain activation revealed by fMRI. Neuroimage 26

Fisher HE (1998). Lust attraction and attachment in mammalian reproduction. Human Nature 9

Fonteille V & Stoleru S. (2010). The cerebral correlates of sexual desire:

Functional neuroimaging approach. Sexologies 10.1016/j.sexol.2010.03.011.

Francoeur, Robert T. (1991). "Sexual Desire and Love Play." In Becoming a Sexual Person. New York: Macmillan Publishing Company.

Frayser, S. G. (1985). Varieties of sexual experience: An anthropological perspective on human sexuality. New Haven, CT: Human Relations Area Files Press.

Frayser, S. G. (1994). Defining normal childhood sexuality: An anthropological approach. Annual Review of Sex Research, 5, 173-217.

Freedman, Estelle & John D'Emilio. (1988) Intimate Matters: A History of Sexuality in America. New York: Harper and Row.

Fruth, B. and Hohmann, G. (2006) Social grease for females? Same-sex genital contacts in wild bonobos. In Homosexual Behaviour in Animals

(Sommer, V. and Vasey, P.L., eds), pp. 294–315, Cambridge University Press

Gathorne-Hardy, Jonathan. (1998). Sex the Measure of All Things. London: Chatto & Windus.

Giammanco, M., G. Tabacchi, et al. (2005). "Testosterone and aggressiveness." Med Sci Monit 11 (4)

Giedd, J. (2005). Personal communication. Giedd, J. N. (2003). "The anatomy of mentalization: A view from developmental neuroimaging." Bull Menninger Clin 67

Goldberg, Vicki. (January 21, 2001). "A Peek Inside Kinsey's Cabinet." The New York Times, 47-48.

Groneman, Carol. (2000). Nymphomania: A History. New York: W. W. Norton & Company.

Hemanth P. Nair and Larry J. Young "Vasopressin and Pair-Bond

Formation: Genes to Brain to Behavior" Physiology Published 1 April 2006 Vol. 21 no. 2, DOI: 10.1152/physiol.00049.2005

Haith MM, Bergman T, Moore MJ. Eye contact and face scanning in early infancy. Science. 1977.

Hrdy, S. B. (1997). "Raising Darwin's consciousness: Female sexuality and the prehominid origins of patriarchy." Human Nature 8

Halpern, Carolyn J, et al. (2000). "Adolescent males' willingness to report masturbation." The Journal of Sex Research, 37(4), 327-332.

Harrison, Daniel M. (2002). "Rethinking Circumcision and Sexuality in the United States." Sexualities, 5(3), 303–4.

Herdt, G. H. (1997). Same sex, different cultures. Boulder, CO: Westview Press.

Hurlbert, David F. & Karen E. Whittaker. (1991). "The Role of Masturbation in Marital and Sexual Satisfaction: A Comparative Study of Female Masturbators and nonmasturbators."Journal of Sex Education and Therapy, 17(4): 272–282.

Huber, D., P. Veinante, et al. (2005). "Vasopressin and oxytocin excite distinct neuronal populations in the central amygdala." Science 308

Hultcrantz, M. (2006). "Estrogen and hearing: A summary of recent investigations." Acta Otolaryngol 126

Hamann S Herman RA Nolan CL & Wallen K (2004). Men and women differ in amygdala response to visual sexual stimuli. Nature Neuroscience 7.

Hatfield E & Sprecher S. (1986). Measuring passionate love in intimate relationships. Journal of Adolescence 9

Hatfield E. Love, Sex and Intimacy. New York: Harper Collins 1993.

Heaton JP, Adams MA. Update on central function relevant to sex: remodeling the basis of drug treatments for sex and the brain. Int J Impot Res 2003.

Insel TR and Hulihan TJ. A gender-specific mechanism for pair bonding: oxytocin and partner preference formation in monogamous voles. Behav Neurosci 109, 1995.CrossRefMedlineWeb of Science

Neumann ID. Brain oxytocin: A key regulator of emotional and social behaviours in both females and males. J Neuroendocrinol. 2008.

Insel TR and Shapiro LE. Oxytocin receptor distribution reflects social organization in monogamous and polygamous voles. Proc Natl Acad Sci USA 89, 1992.

Insel TR, Wang ZX, and Ferris CF. Patterns of brain vasopressin receptor distribution associated with social organization in microtine rodents. J Neurosci 14, 1994.

Johnson, James R. (1982). "Toward a Biblical Approach to Masturbation." Journal of Psychology and Theology, 10(2): 137–146.

Kellogg, J. H. (1888). Plain Facts for Old and Young: Natural History and Hygiene of Organic Life. Burlington, IA: I.F. Segner.

Kinsey, Alfred C., Wardell B. Pomeroy, Clyde E. Martin, & Paul H. Gebhard. (1953). Sexual Behavior in the Human Female. Philadelphia: W. B. Saunders Company.

Kinsey, Alfred C., Wardell B. Pomeroy, and Clyde E. Martin. (1948). Sexual Behavior in The Human Male. Philadelphia: W. B. Saunders Company.

Komisaruk BR, Whipple B. Love as sensory stimulation: physiological consequences of its deprivation and

expression.
Psychoneuroendocrinology 1998.

Kuels, Eva C. (1985). The Reign of the Phallus. Berkeley: University of California Press.

Laumann, Edward O., John H. Gagnon, Robert T. Michael, & Stuart Michaels. (1994). The Social Organization of Sexuality: Sexual Practices in the United States. Chicago: The University of Chicago Press.

Litten, Harold. (1993). The Joy of Solo Sex. Mobile, AL: Factor Press.

LoPiccolo, Joseph, and W. Charles Lobitiz. (1972). "The Role of Masturbation in the Treatment of Orgasmic Dysfunction." Archives of Sexual Behavior, 2(2), 163-171.

Maravilla KR & Yang CC (2007). Sex and the brain: The role of fMRI for assessment of sexual function and response. International Journal of Impotence Research 19.

Maravilla KR & Yang CC (2008). Magnetic resonance imaging and the female sexual response: Overview of techniques results and future directions. Journal of Sexual Medicine 5.

Masters WH & Johnson VE (1966). Human sexual response. Boston: Little Brown.

Moulier V, Mouras H, Pelegrini-Isaac M, Glutron D, Rouxel R & Grandjean B (2006). Neuroanatomical correlates of penile erection evoked by photographic stimuli in human males. Neuroimage 33.

Martinson, Floyd. (1993). The Sexual Life of Children. Westport, CT: Bergin and Garvey.

Masters, William H., Virginia E. Johnson, & Robert C. Kolodny. (1986). Masters and Johnson on Sex and Human Loving. Boston: Little, Brown and Company.

McNab, Warren. (1993). "Masturbation: The Neglected Topic in Sexuality Education." Family Life Education, 12(2) : 10-15.

Michael, Robert T, John H. Gagnon, Edward O. Laumann, & Gina Kolata. (1994). Sex In America: A Definitive Survey. Boston: Little, Brown and Company.

Moglia, Ronald Filiberti and Jon Knowles, eds. (1997). All About Sex: A Family Resource on Sex and Sexuality. New York: Three Rivers Press.

Mosher, Donald L and Susan G. Vonderheide. (1985). "Contributions of sex guilt and masturbation guilt to women's contraceptive attitudes and use." The Journal of Sex Research, 21(1), 24-39.

Mecklenburger, Ralph. Our Religious Brains. Woodstock, VT: Jewish Lights Publishing, 2012

Moody, Raymond. Life after Life. New York: HarperCollins, 2001

Motherby G. A New Medical Dictionary. 2nd ed. London, 1785

Naskar, Abhijit. "The God Parasite: Revelation of Neuroscience", 2015

Naskar, Abhijit. "Autobiography of God: Biopsy of A Cognitive Reality", 2016

Naskar, Abhijit. "Biopsy of Religions: Neuroanalysis towards Universal Tolerance", 2016

Naskar, Abhijit. "What is Mind?, 2016

Naskar, Abhijit. "In Search of Divinity: Journey to The Kingdom of Conscience", 2016

Naskar, Abhijit. "Love, God & Neurons: Memoir of a scientist who found himself by getting lost", 2016

Naskar, Abhijit. "Neurons of Jesus: Mind of A Teacher, Spouse & Thinker", 2017

Naskar, Abhijit. "Principia Humanitas", 2017

Naskar, Abhijit. "Rowdy Buddha: The First Sapiens", 2017

Newberg, Andrew, and Jeremy Iversen. "The Neural Basis of the Complex Mental Task of Meditation: Neurotransmitter and Neurochemical Considerations." Medical Hypotheses 61, no. 2 (2003)

Newberg, Andrew, and Mark Waldman. How God Changes Your Brain. New York: Ballantine, 2010

Newberg, Andrew, and Stephanie Newberg. "A Neuropsychological Perspective on Spiritual Development." In Handbook of Spiritual Development in Childhood and Adolescence, edited by Eugene Roehlkepartain, Pamela King, Linda

Wagener, and Peter Benson. London: Sage Publications, Inc., 2005

O'Doherty JP (2004). Reward representations and reward-related learning in the human brain: Insights from neuroimaging. Current Opinion in Neurobiology 14.

Ortigue S & Bianchi-Demicheli F (2007). Interactions between human sexual arousal and sexual desire: a challenge for social neuroscience. Revue Medicale Suisse 3.

Ortigue S, Bianchi-Demicheli F de C, Hamilton AF & Grafton ST (2007). The neural basis of love as a subliminal prime: An event-related functional magnetic resonance imaging study. Journal of Cognitive Neuroscience 19.

Ortigue S, Bianchi-Demicheli F, Patel N, Frum C & Lewis JW (2010). Neuroimaging of love: fMRI meta-analysis evidence toward new perspectives in sexual medicine. Journal of Sexual Medicine 7.

Ortigue S, Patel N & Bianchi-Demicheli F (2009). New electroencephalogram (EEG) neuroimaging methods of analyzing brain activity applicable to the study of human sexual response. Journal of Sexual Medicine 6.

Onions CT. The Oxford Dictionary of English Etymology. New York: Oxford University Press 1966.

Patton, Michael S. (1985). "Masturbation from Judaism to Victorianism." Journal of Religion and Health, 24(2), 133– 146.

- (1986). "Twentieth-century Attitudes Toward Masturbation." Journal of Religion and Health, 25(4), 291– 302.

Phipps, William E. (1977). "Masturbation: Vice or Virtue?" Journal of Religion and Health, 16(3), 183–195.

Pomeroy, Sarah B. (1975). Goddesses, Whores, Wives, and Slaves: Women in Classical Antiquity. New York: Schocken Books.

Pomeroy, Wardell. (1968). Boys and Sex. New York: Delacorte Press.

- (1969). Girls and Sex. New York: Delacorte Press.

Ranke-Heinemann, Uta. (1990). Eunuchs For the Kingdom of Heaven: Women, Sexuality, and the Catholic Church. Translated by Peter Heinegg. New York: Doubleday.

Rashkow, Ilona N. (2000). Taboo or Not Taboo: Sexuality and Family in the Hebrew Bible. Minneapolis, MN: Fortress Press.

Renshaw, Domeena C. (1976). "Understanding Masturbation." Journal of School Health, 46(2), 98–101.

Redoute J, Stoleru S, Gregoire MC, Costes N, Cinotti L, Lavenne F et al.

(2000). Brain processing of visual sexual stimuli in human males. Human Brain Mapping 11.

Redoute Jr M, Stolery S, Gregoire M-C, Costes N, Cinotti L, Lavenne F et al. (2000). Brain processing of visual sexual stimuli in human males. Human Brain Mapping 11.

Regan PC (1998). Of lust and love: Beliefs about the role of sexual desire in romantic relationships. Personal Relationships 5.

Rieger G, Bailey JM & Chivers ML (2005). Sexual arousal patterns of bisexual men. Psychological Science 16.

Rowan, Edward L. (2000). The Joy of Self-Pleasuring. New York: Prometheus Books.

Rydström, Jens. (2000) "'Sodomitical Sins are Threefold': Typologies of Bestiality, Masturbation, and Homosexuality in Sweden," 1880–

1950. Journal of the History of Sexuality, 9(3), 240–276.

Stein, Daniel S. (2000). Passionate Sex. New York: Carroll & Graf Publishers.

Stengers, Jean & Anne Van Neck. (2001) Masturbation: The History of a Great Terror. New York: Palgrave/St. Martins.

Stevenson, David. (2000). Recording the Unspeakable: Masturbation in the Diary of William Drummond, 1657–1659. Journal of the History of Sexuality, 9(3), 223–239.

Stolberg, Michael. (January/April 2000). "Self-Pollution, Moral Reform, and the Venereal Trade: Notes On the Sources and Historical Context of Onania (1716)." Journal of the History of Sexuality, 9(1–2), 37–61.

Thompson EM & Morgan EM (2008). "Mostly straight" young women: Variations in sexual behavior and identity development. Developmental Psychology 44.

Uvnas-Moberg K, Petersson M. [Oxytocin, a mediator of antistress, well-being, social interaction, growth and healing] Z Psychosom Med Psychother. 2005;51.

Van Roosmalen, J., & Rosendaal, F. (2002). There is still room for disagreement about vaginal delivery of breech infants at term. BJOG, 109.

van de Walle, B. (1965). "Egypt: Syncretism and State Religion." In Pierre Grimal, ed., Larousse World Mythology. New York: Prometheus Press.

Veyne, Paul. (1987). "The Roman Empire." The History of Private Life — I, From Pagan Rome to Byzantium. Cambridge, MA: Belknap Press, 5–206.

Whyte, H., Hannah, M. E., Saigal, S., Hannah, W. J., Hewson, S., Amankwah, K., et al. (2004). Outcomes of children at 2 years after planned cesarean birth versus planned vaginal birth for breech presentation at term: The international randomized term breech trial. Am J Obstet Gynecol, 191(3).

Walter M, Bermpohl F, Mouras H, Schiltz K, Tempelmann C, Rotte M et al. (2008). Distinguishing specific sexual and general emotional effects in fMRI-subcortical and cortical arousal during erotic picture viewing. Neuroimage 40.

Weinberg MS, Williams CJ & Pryor DW (1994). Dual attraction: Understanding bisexuality. Oxford University Press, New York.

Xu X, Aron A, Brown L, Cao G, Feng T & Weng X (2010). Reward and motivation systems: A brain mapping study of early-stage intense romantic love in Chinese participants. Human Brain Mapping 32.

Young, Larry J. "The Neural Basis of Pair Bonding in a Monogamous Species: A Model for Understanding the Biological Basis of Human Behavior" Offspring: Human Fertility Behavior in Biodemographic Perspective. National Academies Press (US); 2003.

Young, Larry J. and Wang, Z. "The neurobiology of pair bonding" Nature Neuroscience 7 (2004)

Zilbergeld, Bernie. (1992). The New Male Sexuality. New York: Bantam Books.

EITHER CIVILIZED OR PHOBIC

www.ingramcontent.com/pod-product-compliance
Lightning Source LLC
Chambersburg PA
CBHW020514290526
45786CB00002B/601